CONCILIUM

CONCILIUM 2021/2

Synodalities

Edited by

Michel Andraos, Thierry-Marie Courau OP,
and Carlos Mendoza Álvarez OP

Published in 2021 by SCM Press, 3rd Floor, Invicta House, 108–114 Golden Lane, London EC1Y 0TG.

SCM Press is an imprint of Hymns Ancient & Modern Ltd (a registered charity)
13A Hellesdon Park Road, Norwich NR6 5DR, UK

www.concilium.in

ISBN 978-0-334-03158-1

Concilium is published in March, June, August, October, December

Contents

Editorial

Since the Second Vatican Council and under its influence, synodical practices have been developing at various levels within the Church: in Papal practices, at the Diocesan level and within ecclesiastical communities. Society is also seeking new ways to govern itself. Pope Francis deliberately chose to take a personal interest in this with regard to both the future of the catholic Church and evangelisation and has organised a synod for the autumn of 2021 on synodality. Its purpose[1] is to turn clearly away from an artificial construct of uniformity set up to further the ends of control and power in order to encourage the distinctive expressions that the Spirit engenders both in today's Church and the world at large. By seeking for truth, by accepting that one should not seek to impose ideas on others nor to discredit them, by renouncing the destruction of any other person or thing, by renouncing the seizure of power to satisfy any self-interest, by embracing the tensions at play between two or more differing points without conflict or confrontation, a greater richness is revealed that will enable us to move forward together founded in difference and nuance. This can happen in a Church which both listens both to the world and its members and which becomes the subject of its story, that is to say of each of its members, without exception, starting with the poorest, the most humble, the most neglected and by sheltering them from the pressures exerted on them by the powerful.

While the vision of a synodical Church is widely shared, as noted in the International Theological Commission's 2018 report, the theological work needs to be pursued in order to clarify the principles and pastoral choices and practitioners need to be unequivocally involved. This edition of Concilium is intended to prepare the ground for this event, so essential to the future of the Catholic Church and to lend support for the implementation of this initiative by the pontiff.

This edition is split into three sections: sharing some examples of synodical practice in the Church across the world; showcasing some biblical, anthropological and practical approaches to synodical practice; putting forward some specific proposals to establish and sustain life and practice in a truly synodical Catholic Church. These eleven articles do not, obviously, pretend either to set out how things are nor offer an exhaustive approach. These are signs inviting the work of synodality to be taken seriously, so it does not stay as a vain hope nor as an ideal of a communion never tried, so it can properly become part of the daily lives of Christians and their Church. A building block and an encouragement for the preparation of the forthcoming synod.

The first section sets out the field of study and reflection drawing on several successful synodical events, both recent and locally based, that have taken place in Latin America, Europe and Asia and, most recently, in Amazonia. **Celia Rojas Chávez,** a sister of the Divine Shepherd, who has lived for the past 27 years amongst the Mayan Tseltal and Tsotsil tribes, recounts the fruits of her lived experience 20 years after the 3rd Diocesan Synod in San Cristóbal de Las Casas, Chiapas (Mexico). She sets out the ecclesiastical experience of the synodality of an indigenous Church within the Mayan context. In the midst of armed conflict, this Church opted to take the poor and the indigenous peoples of Chiapas as its beacon. This enabled it to adopt a pastoral approach founded in justice, choosing the building of justice and peace as signs of the Kingdom of God.

Professor of Dogmatics in the Faculty of Catholic Theology at the University of Erfurt (Germany), **Julia Knop,** and **Martin Kirschner**, Professor of Theology in the Change Processes of Today's World at the Catholic University of Eichstätt-Ingolstadt (Germany) uncover the methods that underpin the synodical practices of the German Church and what they bring to the universal Church. This Church, in dealing with the abuse of power and sexualised violence, takes into account the cultural and underlying structural factors which can make them either possible or encourage them. The exercise of power and sexuality, priests' ways of life and self-perception, women's position in the Church and the search for a shared and transparent form of both self-awareness and the way decisions are taken by the Church are examined within the wider context of the challenges faced by the world, of increasing polarisation and the threats that weigh upon the Church and social unity.

The Indian feminist theologian, **Kochurani Abraham**, Vice President of the Indian Theological Association (ITA), engaged in the field of justice both in practice and the university context, makes a critical analysis of the core theme, "the path of synodality as God would expect in the Church of the third millennium", from the standpoint of Asian and Indian women, in particular. This leads her to show that questions of gender lie at the heart of the process of becoming a synodical Church. The Indian Christian Women's Movement (ICWM), an independent platform bringing to together women of Christian faiths in India, is put forward as a model of synodality in practice, as a new way of being a Church.

Research Professor at the Pontifical Catholic University of Paraná (PUC) at Curitiba (Brazil), expert of the Episcopal Conference of Latin America (CELAM) at the conferences in Santo Domingo in 1992 and Aparecida in 2007 and an assessor of the National Conference of Brazilian Bishops, **Agenor Brighenti**, takes his recent experience of the Amazonian Synod as his starting point. Using this he shows us that a synodical approach is formed in the relationships between global and local, that it lies in the conception of universality as the convergence of diverse characteristics. In so far as it is a new subject and a new paradigm, Amazonia transcends Amazonia. The regional synod has a planetary reach. The periphery has come to the heart of the Church making waves and generating unease. It incites it to realign itself and to welcome the questioning of the Spirit that, in today's Church, comes principally from the southern hemisphere.

The second section deals with the reality of the synodical life of the Church from the perspectives of the Bible, history and ecclesiology. The New Testament exegete, Dominican and President of the Catholic Theological Union of Chicago (USA), **Barbara Reid**, sets out to find approaches in the earliest Christian communities that are intentionally synodical and collegiate in their ways of thinking and doing. Using the Acts of the Apostles, she highlights their practices of collective prayer, communal meals, shared resources and engagement in their mission of evangelism. She studies how the actions of those in charge enabled them able to resolve threats to ecclesiastical harmony. By way of a response she suggests approaches based on modern management science that can shine a light on a dynamically engaged synod.

Professor in African studies and World Christianity at DePaul University, Chicago, (USA) **Stan Chu Ilo,** gives us an introduction into the rich and globally unique world of the social and spiritual heritage of numerous African traditions: "Palaver". It is the art of dialogue, of conversation, of the search for consensus with the objective of deciding to live harmoniously within society. African Christians have this tradition available to them for resolving conflicts, for healing the polarising differences in their churches on matters of faith and morals and for maintaining a dynamic balance between tradition and innovation. The African "Palaver", particularly that of the ethnic Igbo's from western Africa is an example of how a non-western civilisation has developed ways of listening, of discerning the truth of things and of knowing the path to follow to build a shared future. This sacred space for creative dialogue intended for shared decision making where everyone's voices, the concerns and ideas are welcome, could well be a model for designing the synodical approach for which the Church is waiting.

Alphonse Borras, Professor Emeritus of Canon Law at the University of Louvain (Belgium), suggests a reflection upon the questions that putting into practice a proper synodical approach based in Church law and theology raise. Being aware that many Catholics, due to their attachment to the democratic ethos of their societies and the ecclesiastical consciences, feel that they have a right to be heard about their views on the Church and the proclamation of the Gospel, he seeks to go beyond the divide between what would only be a consultative approach and what would only be a matter of debate. He chooses to uphold the shared baptismal responsibility of all those involved in the decision making process as much as he does the freedom of the Minister, guarantor of church unity, to show the extent of the ecclesiastical reach of synodality *in action*. The scope of what is canonically possible is overtaken by respecting the ecclesiastical community's pneumatological dimension.

The third section takes stock and opens up the theological and pastoral perspectives of the issue of the Catholic Church's governance by means of using synodality in action. It sets out a route map. **Gilles Routhier**, Professor at Laval University, Quebec (Canada), President of the Conference of Catholic Theological Institutions (CICT-COCTI), of the International Federation of Catholic Universities (FIUC-IFCU), researcher in ecclesiology and practical theology, highlighted the issue of synodality of local Churches, over thirty years ago. In his article he shows how, because time and again synodality has been called upon and has become a fashionable slogan, we no longer appreciate that it is something innate to the Church itself, that it is an essential characteristic, a dimensional constituent and an expression of the Gospel. Far from being something fashionable, synodality is a fundamental requirement since, by its very nature, the Church is called to fulfilment based on the synodical principle and on the call to live synodically. The author calls the Church not only to live according to the present times but also to become, through a process of permanent conversion, what in reality it is.

Professor of Catholic Systematic Theology at Boston College, Boston (USA), **Richard R. Gaillardetz** shows how synodality, a central theme of Pope Francis' theology, casts doubt on a toxic ecclesiastical hierarchy. Considering synodality's theological principles and the key ideas from the teachings of Vatican II, he explores the ways in which synodality can contribute to dealing with the problematical characteristics of hierarchy and clericalism within the ministerial structures of Church governance. For Galliardetz, the conciliatory nature of synodality's theological principles leads us to consider new perspectives on the Church's public ministry, ordained and lay, and to raise questions about the Roman Catholic Church present form of episcopal governance.

Based in Santiago de Chile, the professor and researcher at the Manuel Larrain Theological Centre of the Universidad Alberto Hurtado, **Carlos Schickendantz**, shares some ecclesiological reflections based on a so called "Copernican revolution" from Vatican II about the conception that the Church has of itself. Using examples, he sets out the systemic problems which constitute the obstacles to its transformation as the sacrament of salvation in today's world. In particular, he comments on the scarcely credible context of clerical sexual abuse by clerics and the implied involvement of the institutional hierarchy and how this will take the Church beyond any sense of benevolent naivety regarding the innocence of those who oppose its renewal.

Finally, the French Dominican theologian, ecclesiologist and ecumenicist **Hervé Legrand**, honorary Professor of the Institut Catholique de Paris, sets out the route map for practical implementation pleading the cause of learning the lessons of synodality. The scandal of abuse has made clear to everyone the dysfunctionality of an authoritarian and clerical ecclesiology inherited from the 19th Century. The systemic crisis, the sensitivity of which has been heightened by the present rapid societal changes, is leading Pope Francis and theologians to seek remedies through the growth of synodality. The article explores a series of cycles of learning that have allowed lay members to exercise their citizenship through various planned councils and Diocesan synods. It is in these setting that the clergy find their rightful place, their vocation and their ordination placing them *within* the Church and not solely *in front* of it due to a fallacious semi-absorption in Christ and powers that they might exercise as they saw fit.

This edition closes with the theological forum presenting Pope Francis' commitment to a new economy as his latest encyclical *Fratelli tutti* and his most recent work *Ritorniamo a sognare* (Let us dream) both bear witness.

Michel Andraos, Thierry-Marie Courau OP,
Carlos Mendoza-Álvarez OP

Notes

1. Pope Francis, *Un temps pour changer*, Paris, Fayard, 2020

Part One: Experiences of Synodal Practices in World Church

The Third Diocesan Synod of San Cristóbal de Las Casas, Chiapas: A Synodal Experience Inculturated in a Mayan Context

CELIA ROJAS CHÁVEZ

Twenty-five years from the calling and twenty-one years from the conclusion of the Third Diocesan Synod of San Cristóbal de Las Casas, the article presents some features of the Church experience of synodality in a native Church in a Mayan context that made the option for the poor and for the native peoples of Chiapas its banner in the midst of an armed conflict with the aim of pastoral discernment in order to build justice and peace as signs of the Kingdom of God.

I Introduction

The two earlier diocesan synods had their own particular reasons. That of 1908 marked the history of the original evangelisation and in 1947 the rules of Benedict XV's canon law were applied.[1]

When he arrived in the diocese in 1960, *jTatic*[2] Samuel Ruiz García implemented the Second Vatican Council through a process of openness to the Spirit in which we Agents of Pastoral Animation and Coordination (AACP)[3] went through a process of gradual *undoing* of our way of understanding the Church: we learned, together with the communities we accompanied, to start building the Church of Jesus as the Church of the poor. This process required the creation of new ministries, forms of organisation and structures for a community-based Church modelled on the first Christian communities. It implied moving from being a person who said which way to go and what to do, to learning together how to live the faith in the midst of the complex life of the communities.

Living the Christian and Catholic faith in terms of the Second Vatican Council presupposed understanding that the 'joys and hopes' were adopted in pastoral work. The hope of having 'life abundantly', as Jesus tells us, marked our service. Land, education, health care, an economy based on solidarity, justice, resolution of conflicts, women's participation, individual rights and rights of Mother Earth were themes that permeated the reflections provoked by the Word of God and led to a series of actions that strengthened the faith and encouraged a different life. The 1974 Indigenous Congress, the emergence of the role of *tuneles*,[4] the different diocesan commissions or coordinating groups, the sub-teams for pastoral work, the Diocesan Assembly, the Diocesan Pastoral Council, the social organisations that grew out of the Word of God such as the Believing People and other groups, energised the diocese's journey. In this way we gradually built a living Church, with a shared awareness of its defects and rights, but marked above all by growth in social organisation as a Church commitment in favour of life.

On 1 January 1994 the armed uprising of the Zapatista National Liberation Army (EZLN) shook the whole country. The proposals that later gave rise to the dialogues in the Cathedral of Peace – and later in San Andrés – coincided completely with the criticisms repeatedly made by the diocese of San Cristóbal de Las Casas. This period also saw the growth of attacks and slanders against the pastoral work of *jTatic* Samuel and the diocese; the bishop and the AACP were accused of starting the uprising. Such accusations reached the point of calling in question whether *jTatic* Samuel could remain in charge of the diocese. This was the context in which we were summoned to hold the Third Diocesan Synod, not to implement a set of rules or to recapture a history, but to review the work of evangelisation.

Holding a synod in the midst of such difficulties and risks could not be the result of fear of the implications following Jesus, the good shepherd, but of openness to the Spirit. *jTatic* Samuel used to encourage us: 'If from time to time we question our pastoral work, let us review it to make corrections where we went wrong and strengthen our confidence that God supports the diocesan approach and look to see what we have failed to do.'

He defined the process as 'a time to harvest and a time to build'.

Starting this synodal process in the middle of an armed uprising was a huge challenge. Efforts were made to ensure that all the communities could take part: preliminary work was done to get the views of each parish and choose delegates to the Assemblies of Pastoral Region Teams, which in turn would choose delegates to take part in the diocesan synodal assemblies. How could the process start in the midst of the insecurity in which we were living? The presence of the Mexican army had increased in many of our parishes, and there was an atmosphere of intimidation directed at the various community officers. Trusting in the Spirit of God, who does not err when he guides us, however winding the way may appear, we started on the work.

II Sowing the Synod

From 20 July 1994 to 25 January 1995, from the calling of the synod to the beginning of the work for the first synodal assembly, the communities' capacity to respond was on display. As a stage of awareness-raising, as when the land is ready for sowing, a banner and a cross decorated with ribbons went from community to community, calling on each community to pray and prepare for the work, which would take a considerable time. It was a real celebration, with prayers, ritual dancing, celebrations of the Word of God, food and dancing. In all the prayers there were intercessions for *jTatic* Samuel, for our whole threatened diocesan Church and for the problems in each community, always with the hope for a better life.

Together with another sister from my congregation and a Tseltal sister, I accompanied the pastoral process in the parish of Santa Catarina in Pentelho', Chiapas, where there was no resident parish priest. We made a plan to visit the communities in the valley and on the mountain, and only staffed the parish centre at the weekend. This enabled us to be more involved in the synodal process and feel that we were part of living Church, a Church on the move.

There were dialogues between the communities to organise the reception of the symbols. The different servants of the community asked the area leaders and *Tuneles* for support. The total dedication of those responsible for coordinating each of the pastoral areas of the parish became clearer. It is important to stress this because this community service is unpaid, and the area leaders and *Tuneles* had to serve for months, which meant not looking after their maize fields, leaving their children with the family or taking the youngest ones with them, which was always more difficult for pregnant women or those looking after small children.

I took part in two diocesan coordinating groups, Indian Theology and Diocesan deacons' Meetings, as a result of which I was invited to be part of the coordinating group of the First Synodal Assembly. The first subject to be discussed was 'Native Church'. For this first topic and for the other five it was decided to set up the process of Synodal Assemblies in each community, area and region, each parish and pastoral team. It was a real exercise in *co-responsibility* that demonstrated the maturity of the participants and their sense of being part of the Church. The result of various months of reflection, discussion, heartfelt questions and agreements were reflected in the Final Document. In the following paragraphs I shall indicate some of the conclusions that were the harvest of the evangelisation process.

Being a Native Church does not mean being autonomous. Very many of the members of the first peoples were trying to construct their autonomy in the face of a Mexican political and economic system that threatened and continues to put at risk the lives of the communities, but we could not translate this attempt-struggle-construction into the sphere of the Church. The work of the synod made us think about the need for *communion*. This was an obvious challenge in every parish, where ancient wounds persist, caused by contempt for the native people and a breach with some sections of the mixed-race people, since they are the ones that take the political and economic decisions.

The process of Indian Theology in the diocese did not take many years, but it did promote the recovery of the cultural values, wisdom and experience of God of the native peoples. The Synodal Assembly therefore took up the challenge to continue the recovery of the ancestral wealth preserved with much care by the communities. This challenge was to go hand in hand with weaving together Church life out of the cultural riches of the Tsotsil, Tseltal, Ch'ol, and Tojolabal, always taking care to respect the differences.

Being a native Church brings with it the commitment to care for and defend the planet. This involved a change of attitudes that brings us to recover the original harmony sown in our hearts by the Spirit of God, not forgetting that it requires us to work out a position towards the extractive projects that put the accumulation of wealth above the welfare of individuals and peoples.

At the end of the first Synodal Assembly, the communities worked on the second topic, *A Liberating Church*. The hope and strength of the workers in each of the parishes was obvious. These were times of increased military harassment as the official security forces gained ground locally.[5] On more than one occasion delegates to the Pastoral or Team Assemblies were interrogated on their way to meetings, which meant greater care about the documents they carried, because they were carrying details of the local situation analyses, which were a clear condemnation of the violations of the communities' security and peace. The situation of that time was described in the document *The suffering of the people, The people are waking up, A people on the way, In this time of war mediation and reconciliation*.

It is worth remembering that since 1975,[6] when the diocese made its preferential option for the poor, it had become clear that to take this path would mean accepting the consequences of always being on the side of the most disadvantaged. But after the armed uprising the contradictions and confrontations in the communities became sharper, and the Third Diocesan Synod looked again at the challenges posed by such a complex situation. In the section 'In this time of war' we find a definition of 'Christian attitudes in a time of conflict and pastoral ministry in this time of war'.

After this came a time of 'low intensity warfare' on the part of the state and the paramilitaries, but the real sensation was that the conflict was constantly increasing in intensity: military checkpoints, community workers kept under observation, increasing conflicts within communities that resulted in division and exhaustion. As a result, achieving agreement on the need to 'be aware and accept the risks involved in speaking the truth because we know that the truth will set us free,'[7] was what gave us the energy to keep going and, above all, kept our hearts strong in the face of new trials. Other agreements were 'not to fall into the corruption of the system when holding public office..., overcoming fears and taking no notice of criticism..., not harbouring resentment against those who have harmed us.'[8]

This Synodal Assembly made it clear that the experience of increasing persecution and conflicts that led to martyrdom for the first Christians was going to be repeated in our diocese, as section 82 reminds us: 'In times of persecution and conflict, although it is much more difficult, we must stand firm in our mission, not stop attending our meetings,... and even more we must keep alert to rebut with cunning and simplicity whatever may damage our pastoral work.'

Being mostly lay people, the pastoral workers had every right to be involved in politics. Nevertheless the difficulties experienced in the communities as a result of different political involvements led us to reflect on the position of the Church in these circumstances, and we concluded that as a Church we could not be identified with or depend on parties and political or military organisations.

The fact that in 1996 *jTatic* Samuel acted as a mediator in the dialogues between the federal government and the EZLN led the diocesan workers also to carry out this service of mediation and reconciliation at community level, so that a new characteristic of the diocesan worker was identified in each community. It was formulated in paragraph 91: 'To achieve reconciliation we shall search for peaceful solutions... through dialogue, knowing that we are acting in terms of the Church's mission as mediators of peace.'

At the end of the Second Synodal Assembly it was becoming clear that the complex situation throughout the territory of the diocese required processes of personal and community conversion and a deep experience of prayer to implore the God of life to 'give more wisdom and more strength to our hearts to be able to guide us'.[9]

With all the riches and the questions that remained in our hearts after the first two Synodal Assemblies we explored further our identity as an *Evangelising Church.* This Assembly was very dense because of the topics we had to deal with, which were recorded in over two hundred paragraphs of the Final Document. By this time the process of the Children's Synod had already started in the diocese; its proceedings are an appendix to the documents of the Third Diocesan Synod. The Assembly of the Believing People was recognised in the Third Diocesan Synod for its participation in the situation analysis of the communities in the light of the Word of God,[10] for its proposals for actions that in most cases solved the process of access to justice for the members of the diocese or people from other places who applied to the coordinating group of the Believing People for support in reporting the sufferings, pain and distress to which they had been subjected.[11] Since then the Believing People's presence in the communities has grown. Every year it organises a huge pilgrimage on 25 January for the anniversaries of the episcopal ordination and the Passover of *jTatic* Samuel Ruiz García at which the injustices experienced in the communities are denounced and there is a sharing of the hopes that maintain the faith of the believers and the pastoral workers of the diocese.[11]

III By way of conclusion

This account does not do justice to our memories of our experience of the whole synodal process. Nevertheless I cannot help but recognise that it is a gift from God to be part of a community of pastoral workers.

Twenty years after the holding of the Third Diocesan Synod, there is still much to be done if the invitations from God presented in the Final Document are to be made a reality. The following are some of the challenges I think are most important:

- To maintain the freshness of the face of our particular Church since the Third Diocesan Synod when a good many of the pastoral workers, including the full-time lay staff, did not experience the synodal process and some have not studied the Final Document and its implications.
- To ensure that we follow the mechanisms by which the different ministries and services that have come into being through this whole process nurture the character of a native and liberating Church, maintain the system under which the pastoral workers are nominated and/or elected by the communities, evaluated at agreed intervals, and confirmed in post or removed as appropriate.
- While it is true that the liturgies and celebrations increasingly display the riches sown by God in the native peoples, it is necessary to take further the process of inculturation in our diocese and expand it to the different peoples and cultures that are part of it.
- Accompaniment for the faithful remnant, the pastoral workers and the believing community that continues its journey in the spirit of the Third Diocesan Synod, and support for their participation in social or political

organisations that strive for a decent life in the midst of so many political divisions and options that do not necessarily respect personal dignity - some of these exist even in the remotest communities.

• Strengthen the participation of women at area, parish and diocesan level. Continue support for them and the training that will allow them to be more confident in taking on roles the community assigns to them despite the patriarchal attitudes that still exist even among Church workers.

• The work of evangelisation in the communities where regular migration of young people and adults leads to the acquisition of different and sometimes negative values that can even change cultural patterns and create expectations that do not necessarily benefit the building of the Kingdom.

• Support for communities that have been fragmented and weakened by the volume of welfare payments and partisan policies present in the communities, especially when this creates confrontations between pastoral workers and faithful with different visions and options.

• Living in communion as a Church alongside other Church movements that have come to the diocese with a different way of being the Church of Jesus and avoid the realities of being disciples of Jesus in history.

• Continue to listen carefully to the people of God, practise discernment in teams and together take the decisions that affect the whole diocese. Promote the spirit and practice of the synods that have encouraged participation in pastoral decisions in all areas of pastoral work.

Finally, grow in awareness that harmony with creation necessarily involves the defence of natural resources and the territory and that being a Native Church depends on this.

Translated by Francis McDonagh

Bibliography

Pedro Arriaga, 'Desentrañando a la 'Madre Tierra', *Sal Terrae* 100 (2012), 977-989.

Diócesis de San Cristóbal de Las Casas. *Acuerdos del III Tercer Sínodo Diocesano*, San Cristóbal de Las Casas, 2000.

Enriqueta Lerma, *Los otros creyentes. Territorio y teopraxis de la Iglesia liberadora en la Región Fronteriza de Chiapas*, San Cristóbal de Las Casas, 2019.

Gabriela Robledo, 'Los dominicos y la construcción de una iglesia maya en Chiapas y Guatemala', *Investigación crítica (i+c)*. Year III, No. 5 (July-December 2016), 59-78.

Samuel Ruíz García, *Mi trabajo pastoral en la Diócesis de San Cristóbal de las Casas: principios teológicos*, Mexico City, 1999.

Jorge Valtierra-Zamudio, 'En busca de la Iglesia autóctona: la nueva pastoral indígena en las cañadas tojolabales', *Revista LiminaR. Estudios Sociales y Humanísticos*, Year 10, vol. X, No. 2 (July-December 2012), 74-89.

Notes

1. Diócesis de San Cristóbal de Las Casas, *Acuerdos del III Tercer Sínodo Diocesano*, San Cristóbal de Las Casas, 2000, Presentación, p. 10. In future cited as *III Sínodo Diocesano*.
2. A Mayan term meaning 'Father' or 'Daddy', used by the indigenous communities as a mark of respect.
3. A term used by the Third Diocesan Synod for people who work full-time in the various pastoral processes.
4. *Tunel* means 'servant' in Tseltal. It is used for those who undergo a process of service and preparation leading up to the permanent indigenous diaconate.
5. The so-called Mixed Operational Bases were set up. These were camps where various forces, Public Security, Mexican Army and Criminal Police, formed a single team.
6. Jorge Santiago said of this event: 'One of the important events in the history of the diocese is the Diocesan Pastoral Review Meeting held on 26-28 November 1985, which later became known as the First Diocesan Assembly. At that First Assembly Don Samuel made the following proposal: "Adopting an attitude of searching is the path of the Gospel, and in this process the search is directed towards the oppressed and towards the poor… We talk about an option because we recognise an institutional sin, since we are part of a structure that is also oppressive, in a particular social class within the Church of God. That is why we have to make an option. In making this option we have to begin a journey, a journey that will give us the answer to two situations, the poor, to whom the Gospel is addressed, and the Gospel interpreted from that situation, from the position of the poor, who mediate salvation to us… It is an option in which I can calculate, here and now, the consequences it has, and I think all of us are also making that calculation at this moment."' Cf Jorge Santiago, *La búsqueda de la libertad*, San Cristóbal de Las Casas, 2018, pp. 63-64.
7. III Sínodo Diocesano, *Iglesia Liberadora. En este tiempo de guerra*, p. 54, paragraph e.
8. III Sínodo Diocesano, *Iglesia Liberadora. En este tiempo de guerra*, pp 54-55, paragraphs f.i.j.

9. III Sínodo Diocesano. *Iglesia Liberadora,* 'Mediación y Reconciliación', p. 62, paragraph 97.
10. *Iglesia Liberadora* p. 102, paragraph 235.
11. *Iglesia Liberadora,* p.232.
12. The decisions of the Third Diocesan Synod were endorsed by the coadjutor bishop Don Raúl Vera López OP from 1995 to 1999, when he was removed from his post for his clear support for the pastoral decisions encouraged by *jTatik* Samuel Ruiz. Jorge Santiago says of this: 'On 6 January 2000, the coordinating group of the Diocesan Assembly of the Diocese reported its agreements with sadness and hope: "As a diocese we reaffirm the fundamental options that inspire our life and work and, although we are saddened at being deprived of the worthy successor of Don Samuel, whom the Pope himself gave us, we are united in maintaining the solid hope that the Kingdom of God will continue to grow in the midst of his people, since we believe firmly that behind immediate events is God, who, through the cross and triumph of Christ, looks on us with love and foresight, even if at times we cannot yet clearly understand his plans.' The declaration of the Diocesan Assembly was published in the diocesan Newsletter *El Caminante*, No 31 (17 January 2000).

The Synodal Path of the Church in Germany and its Significance for the Worldwide Church

JULIA KNOP & MARTIN KIRSCHNER

The synodal path of the Church in Germany is of great importance to the universal Church both because of the topics it deals with and as a process. As a response to the scandals caused by the misuse of power and sexualised violence, it considers the underlying cultural and structural factors that have encouraged abuse and made it possible. How to deal with power and sexuality, the life and self-understanding of priests, the position of women in the Church, and working towards a participatory and transparent form of agreement and decision-making in the Church are key themes of Church renewal that can no longer be avoided. The article sets these questions in the wider context of global challenges, increasing polarisation and threats to the unity of Church and society.

I An exchange of letters between Rome and Germany

On 29 June 2019 Catholics in German received mail from the Vatican. Pope Francis wrote directly 'to the pilgrim people of God in Germany'.[1] Such an action is unusual. What had happened?

The Pope himself refers to the *ad limina* visit of the German bishops to Rome. Behind this is the 'synodal path' on which the German bishops conference and the Central Committee of German Catholics, as a representative of the diocesan councils, associations and leading figures among German lay Catholics, had agreed.[2] This process was a reaction to the deep crisis of the Catholic Church exposed in scandals over the abuse of power, sexualised violence and its cover-up, which became so virulent especially in 2010 after the revelations of sexual violence at the Canisius College in Berlin[3] and in 2018 after the publication of the MHG study on sexual abuse by clergy under the responsibility of the German bishops conference, that the credibility, identity and unity of the Church were threatened. A dialogue process was first initiated in 2010 with the main aim of creating a new culture of discussion in the Church supported by all parties. In contrast, the 'synodal path' makes explicit the difficult issues that have for years blocked understanding and agreement within the Church. In the meantime it has become clear that they can no longer be avoided since they concern structural and cultural factors that have encouraged abuse. The issues include the exercise of power in the Church and the demand for participation and transparency, the way of life and role of priests, Church attitudes to sexuality and sexual diversity, and the position of women in the Church. Since such subjects are often polarising and many groups are attempting to prevent open discussion of them, it is possible that opponents of the synodal path acted in the background to push the Pope to intervene in this way.

In his letter Pope Francis gives expression to his concern for the Church in Germany, but he also broadens his view to include the broader, general crisis of our time, as he did in *Evangelii Gaudium* (24.11.2013), *Laudato Si'* and *Veritatis Gaudium* (08.12.2017) in the context of the situation of refugees, the Amazon Synod and now in the context of the coronavirus crisis, identifying the central challenge for both the Church and humanity: 'We all realise that we are not merely living in a time of change, but at a change of epochs, which throws up new and old questions in the face of which a discussion is justified and necessary.'

Against this background the Pope develops his letter from his Easter meditations on the Acts of the Apostles. In the face of the cross and Holy Saturday, 'when the disciples seemed to have lost everything', he points to the Easter message 'from the mouth of a woman' that leads to the Easter joy of an outward-facing Church 'totally permeated by the new life given by the Holy Spirit'. In other words, he definitely does not agree with the apocalyptic tones of the prophets of doom who interpret the synod initiatives in Germany as a symptom of apostasy and a crypto-Protestant self-secularisation of a Church dependent on the state for its survival that is trying to force a liberal reform agenda on to the worldwide Church.[5]

Instead he interprets the current transformations and in particular the crises in the Church as a *kairos* for a fundamental conversion, a turning to the Gospel and to the margins, for a renewal of the 'outward-facing Church' he had sketched out programmatically in *Evangelii Gaudium*.

The synodal path in Germany is first an opening up of a local Church, but it deals with problems and challenges that are not limited to Germany but found everywhere in the worldwide Church. This process is being carefully observed. Interest centres on the topics, but also on the way in which it is being carried out. However much at the moment there is talk about synodal processes and encouragement to engage in them, it is also clear that in the Roman Catholic context the decision-making processes have been thought of so far in terms of hierarchical authority, while synodality as the expression of the community of the whole people of God on its journey has remained limited to formal consultation processes. The synodal path in Germany is exploring a significantly stronger participatory format, in which bishops, experts and the faithful, that is, the so-called 'laity', come together, consult and decide together. For a synodal assembly to take a decision, a threefold two-thirds majority is necessary, of the plenary, of the bishops and – if requested – of women. In this way a more extensive model of synodal catholicity is being developed and practised. Some take hope from this, because they have the same problems in their local Church, but not the comparable resources to deal with them. Others are worried – and at the polarised edges of the Church things are getting stormy and some scent – and tweet – conspiracy. No wonder that this synodal experiment is also seen as (Church) politics and attracting worldwide attention.

II The wider context: challenges of our time

The synodal path of the Catholic Church in Germany has a clearly defined occasion and task: it has to identify the systemic background to sexual, psychological and spiritual abuse by clergy, and the structures that allowed the cover-up and denial of such violence, to analyse them and to correct them. This is what gives the process its force and limits. However, this specific set of tasks runs up against fundamental ecclesiological questions that can no longer be avoided. The process is thus clearly focused, but structurally and in terms of content part of a wider context and naturally feeds back into that.

a) The wider context is formed by the challenges of a world society that is at once globalised and deeply divided, in which an unprecedented expansion of power, wealth and technical possibilities is accompanied by the exclusion, marginalisation and rejection as rubbish of whole regions, classes and peoples. Connected with this is the advancing and increasingly irreversible destruction of the basis of life on the planet. This requires rapid, coordinated action inspired by solidarity, but on the contrary produces an increasing polarisation and disintegration of societies, paralysis of international organisations and the increasing dominance of (self-) destructive strategies including an escalation of violence. Efforts to achieve synodal church agreement are part of this wider human context and, from the perspective of the Kingdom of God must encourage communication, cooperation and integration.

b) The conflicts, power inequalities and polarisations that affect society are reflected in the Church. They come to a head in hostilities over Church politics and theology that have to do with the interpretation of the faith, relationships with the principles of modernity and the increasingly plural processes of late modernity and the associated models of Church and styles of action. The crisis of religion and Church, the increasing erosion of tradition and exclusion of religion from culture, not only in eastern Europe, come up against experiences of perplexity and helplessness. They not only intensify the series of unresolved conflicts over interpretation but are also linked to contrary temptations to relapse into either resignation or excessive adaptation, to construct a fundamentalist identity or to withdraw self-righteously into one's own group.

c) This leads to a third set of problems, rooted in an insufficient reception and development of Vatican II and associated with polarisation within the Church, blocking of reforms, the banning of controversial topics and the exclusion of innovation. In the German context this has to do not only with conflicts over *Humanae Vitae*, the autonomy of academic theology, the authorisation to teach of individual theologians, but particularly about the inadequate reception and development of the Würzburg Synod. The history of synodality in Germany is therefore a history of frustrations, of successive experiences of the ineffectiveness of so many debates on reform and a search for new forms of synodal agreement in the face of restrictive canon law. The great challenges of global justice and the conversion and renewal of the whole Church are overlaid by stale debates about a contemporary understanding of authority, autonomy and participation. In an authoritarian move to establish an identity, traditional views of office, the priestly life, sexual ethics and the relationship of the sexes are being elevated into timeless identity markers of Catholicism. The longer this blocking and identitarian intensification continue, the more unavoidable and at the same time more hopeless seems the resolution of these conflicts. If the Church fails to resolve its internal conflicts, the Church will be unable to contribute to solving the problems of humanity. Reform and (self-) evangelisation go together and cannot be placed in opposition to each other.

III The background: synodal activity and experiences in Germany

The arguments about the renewal of the Church have accompanied the Church since the Council. However, since the phenomenon of decades of violent sexual crimes by clergy covered up by the Church has become obvious throughout the world, and initial analyses have taken place, dealing with these conflicts has become unavoidable. The critical point was reached in Germany in 2010: the dialogue process the German bishops conference started for 2011-2015 under the leadership of Archbishop Zollitsch, is evidence, as is the 2011 theologians' memorandum, of the enormous pressure for action, but, since the difficult issues were explicitly excluded, in practice it produced few results. The consequence was more frustration. Benedict XVI's decision, directly after the exposure of various abuse scandals throughout the world – in the USA, Ireland and Germany – to declare 2009/2010 the Year of the Priest caused more distress. His visit to Germany in 2011 and his proclamation of a Year of Faith (2012-2013) had little effect. Very different was the explosion of his resignation and the election of the Argentine Jorge Bergoglio as his successor. In particular, the two synods on the family on 2014 and 2015 in Rome and the post-synodal Apostolic Constitution *Amoris Laetitiae* (19 March 2016) demonstrate an attempt to move beyond the dilemmas of a sexual morality fixated on Catholic identity and the preservation of Church authority through a more strongly integrated pastoral approach, more directed at human beings, the reality of their lives and sensitivity to their situations. The 2018 Amazon synod testifies to a new relationship between the universal Church and the local Church, to intercultural sensitivity, respect for contexts, priority for ecological and social questions of survival, and the situating of the pastoral conversion of the Church and the sensitive Church issues in this context. Instead of dealing directly with the areas of conflict and introducing a change of course in Church policy, Pope Francis' aim is clearly a broad reframing of the conflicts so as to address them in a pastoral approach to people, a change of perspective at the margins and by 'listening to the cry of the poor and the cry of the earth'. These synodal activities at the level of the universal Church have been and are being received with interest and hope in Germany. Whether such a reframing succeeds overall, and whether it is sufficient to solve the pressing internal Church conflicts, remains to be seen. Certainly the physical and mental danger to those under the Church's care requires much more detailed measures, however necessary the great conversion doubtless is.

For the synodal renewal Francis has called for, the pointers to synodal understanding in the local Churches offer encouragement and guidance to the extent that they respond to the different contexts and are rooted in them. It is worthwhile recalling briefly important synodal events in Germany, which form the local church context and background to the currently prominent synodal path.[6] Of crucial importance for the reception of the Council and for the further development of synodal processes was the 1971-1975 Würzburg Synod.[7] It was a unique event. In often tense discussions between different positions, bishops, lay representatives, theologians and the public jointly took responsibility for the future of the Church in Germany. In the document *Unsere Hoffnung* (Our Hope), they defined their position in programmatic terms in the perspective of hope for the Kingdom of God in responsibility for the universal Church, ecumenical community and with particular responsibility vis à vis Judaism. In the practical reception and at most partial implementation of many synod decisions, it has to be admitted that we see the ambivalence of German synodal experiences and expectations. The synod made possible a good experience of a frank discussion and shared responsibility of office-holders, theologians and the people of God. Authoritarian interventions from Rome, on the other hand, which stifled key aims and reforms at birth, caused enormous frustration. This dialectic of opening up and disappointment left its mark on subsequent developments in Germany.

In East Germany the pastoral synod in Dresden (1973-1975) and the previous Meißen synod (1969-1971) had been very important for the life of the Church in the German Democratic Republic. Despite the pressure of the system of 'real existing socialism' they made it possible to have experiences of being on the move together as Christians in the GDR, to express the faith and to be noticed internationally. While reception within the Church was slight here too, the process developed into wider ecumenical initiatives and into the movements for Justice, Freedom and the Preservation of Creation that made an important contribution to the peaceful revolution of 1989.[8] Perhaps this allows us to record a second important German experience, that the synod process itself – frankness (*parrhesia*), the experience of community and discussion that is prepared for conflict and can cope constructively with it in the context of a common faith and its liturgical celebration – possesses a value of its own that makes itself felt even and especially where freedom is restricted and participation is disregarded, whether in society or in the Church.

IV The synodal path of the Catholic Church in Germany: its wishes...

The synodal path of the Catholic Church in Germany, as was already mentioned, is not seen as a panacea. Instead it is a way for Catholics to react in a focused way to the systemic deficits and dissonances in the Church's attitude and the realities of the Church, which have become impossible to overlook. These factors did not cause the sexualised abuse of vulnerable people by clergy, but did make it possible under the protection of the institution and made it difficult to punish. The findings of the MHG study were shocking: in the period examined, 1946-2014, documentary proof was found in the files of around 5% of diocesan priests, that is, in the files of every twentieth priest, that he had been accused of sexually abusing a minor. This is merely a lower limit, since considerable defects, and even falsification, has been found in diocesan record-keeping. The study highlighted specifically Catholic factors that encouraged abuse by clergy: a precarious attitude to power in the Church, which was vested exclusively in men under vows of celibacy, and 'ambivalent statements and attitudes in Catholic sexual morality with regard to homosexuality'. The research team also recommended that 'the significance of celibacy should be discussed'.

On all these issues many lay people had for long talked about the need for reflection and renewal, but their clear wish had hitherto not started any serious reform process. Now, however, an external academic view had identified a particular potential danger of sexualised violence and abuse of power. It could no longer be evaded. The image of the priest in the Church, the image of women, rules of sexual ethics and the condemnation or avoidance of the issue of homosexuality, all had to be examined. This was necessary because they supported a system in which the physical and mental integrity of boys, girls and (religious) women had been massively damaged and could suffer further harm.

The synodal path took on this challenge. After an initial inaugural plenary assembly at the beginning of 2020 four forums began work. In groups of around 35 people – bishops, priests and laity and experts from various disciplines – the issues of power and the distribution of authority in the Church, sexual morality, priestly life and women in ministries and offices were studied. Analyses were produced and specific proposals were produced to correct problematic Church structures, and for a review of ecclesiology and Church life. These were agreed by the synod assembly. Implementing the measures is up to local bishops, and in some points at least is dependent on Roman agreement. The idea is not simply to produce suggestions that could be implemented within existing canon law and simply require some goodwill on the part of the competent authority. The point was to go further and identify where reform and correction was needed, and this requires agreement from the universal Church.

Because of the restrictions introduced as a result of the COVID-19 pandemic, the originally planned process, which was to last two years with a total of four plenary sessions, has been extended by six months; instead of the synod assembly fixed for September 2020 there is an intermediate phase, with five decentralised regional conferences, intended to pick up the current situation both in terms of process and issues, and keep the conversation going.

VI ...and its significance for the universal Church

What can the synodal path of a local Church achieve, what universal and theological significance can be attributed to it? There are three possible levels:

The Catholic Church's synodal path is relevant to the universal Church because it takes up an issue whose explosive character for the universal Church is undeniable: sexualised abuse by clergy and the underlying Church mentalities and structures – 'clericalism' in short – that do not effectively enough prevent and punish such acts of violence but instead encourage a priestly self-image that can damage others spiritually, physically and psychologically.

The Catholic Church's synodal path is also relevant to the universal Church because of its *format*. Here we have a form of synodality being tried out that can help the existing understanding and the translation of synodal events and structures into canon law to develop further. Even the latest paper from the International Theological Commission on *Synodality in the Life and Mission in the Church* (2 March 2018) merely distinguishes synodality as a listening attitude of the whole Church, and mentions local and universal synodal bodies and structures and major synodal events such as the particular councils and regional synods defined in canon law, the Roman synod of bishops and, of course, councils, A common feature of all these levels is a strict vertical authority. Consultation and decision-making processes are strictly separated in time and personnel. The involvement of local Churches, theologians and the laity does not take place systematically, and has not been translated into a solid canonical form. The idea of a *communio hierarchica* in which ultimately only the ordained ministry decides continues to dominate and block a 'mixed constitution' based on the ecclesiology of Vatican II in which various *loci theologici* are taken into account and the various charisms, competences and organs of the people of God are represented. The synodal path is meant to reflect this better: among the 230 delegates a third are bishops and a third women. A mere half consists of clergy. Even if there is nothing like a proportionate representation of the people of God, the composition and the communications ground rules have already had a lasting impact on the consultations. In connection with the diverse quorums for taking decisions, new experiences of participatory decision-making and leadership culture have been possible. The design of the process has also had an influence: instead of meeting all together in a closed group for three weeks, as happens in the Roman synod of bishops, here synodal formats have been experienced and tried out in various steps over two and a half years.

The synodal path of the Catholic Church in Germany is finally relevant to the universal Church because here a local Church has become active, one that has access to resources at a level available to few other local Churches, there is an organised lay Catholicism embodied in the Central Committee of German Catholics with a history of 170 years, representing large sections of Catholics in associations, which promotes a culture of participation and democratic opinion surveys in the Church. There is also a strong academic theology that, because of its institutional underpinning in state universities practises a culture of academic freedom, interdisciplinary dialogue and critical loyalty to Church institutions. There are also numerous experts from other fields willing to engage in such a Church experiment and contribute to it, and overall a solid culture of democratic virtues in which Catholics in Germany have had much practice and which shapes their expectations for communication and decision-making. On all three levels – focused on issues, innovative in formats and strong in competences – the Catholic Church in Germany has something to give to the universal Church; it can stimulate, share prior experiences and as a part of the whole practise the freedom of speech the Holy Spirit encourages in the whole Church.

These are considerable resources, but they are necessary because the challenges are great – and go far beyond Germany.

- Will it be possible to achieve agreement in faith on controversial topics overlaid with issues of identity and power in view of the increasing polarisation in Church and society? That would be an important contribution to understanding in society, since in the end from dealing with power, questions of gender justice to questions of identity and recognition of differences, it is the same issues that split Church and society.
- Will it be possible to translate such an agreement into binding decisions and conclusions? Only if dialogue and theological insights can be turned into structures and legal regulations can the blockades be

> lifted, and new energies and credibility be released. This comes with the challenge, on the one hand to work out solutions for the specific situation in Germany, but also to feed these in and mediate them to the universal Church. Preserving the unity of the Catholic Church does not mean adherence to the status quo but working together on the processes of a synodal and missionary renewal of the Church such as Pope Francis is constantly calling for. The interplay of the local Churches with the Pope and a renewed Church must show how synodality can be further developed, or perhaps now is the time to prepare for a new Council.

When the Pope in his letter 'to the pilgrim people of God in Germany' mentions the original situation of the first apostolic communities, he makes it clear that the synodal path, like other synodal processes around the world, is not just about individual measures or arguments about Church policy, but about the newness and renewal that comes from the proclamation of the Gospel and living faith.[9] Only if the specific problems, abuses and possibilities for action are faced and confronted with the Gospel, can such newness happen and (self-)evangelisation be taken seriously as a key criterion. A working paper for the synodal way put it like this:

The current crisis of the Church contains a chance of renewal – a constitutional moment in which the people of God, in the face of the existential pressure of the problems and the recognition of the need for change and the possibility of change, accepts its responsibility for pressing forward with the reform process with the bishops. It does so in the hope and confidence that in this process of renewal it will be filled with the Holy Spirit.[10]

Translated by Francis McDonagh

Notes

1. Vgl. http://www.vatican.va/content/francesco/de/letters/2019/documents/papa-francesco_20190629_lettera-fedeligermania.html [Accessed 08/02/2021].
2. Vgl. https://www.synodalerweg.de /[Accessed 08/02/2021]
3. On this, see the first independent report (May 2010) on cases of sexual abuse in schools and other German Jesuit establishments: https://canisius.de/wp-content/uploads/bericht_27_05_2010_ueber_faelle_sexuellen_missbrauchs_an_jesuiteneinrichtungen.pdf

[Accessed 08/02/2021]

4. The full text of the final report, Sexueller Missbrauch an Minderjährigen durch katholische Priester, Diakone und männliche Ordensangehörige im Bereich der Deutschen Bischofskonferenz, can be accessed here: https://www.dbk.de/fileadmin/redaktion/diverse_downloads/dossiers_2018/MHG-Studie-gesamt.pdf [18.08.2020].

5. In rightwing Catholic publications and internet sites in the United States Cardinal Marx and the synodal path have for a long time been blown up into hate figures. Among the more intellectually respectable polemics is George Weigel's articles in *First Things* in which, in increasingly strong language, he accuses the German Church of apostasy and of being in a de facto schism, and instead of reforms and dialogue argues for Catholic teaching and piety that seamlessly fits his own position in Church politics: 'Much of the Catholic Church in Germany (and in other German-speaking lands) is in a de facto state of schism: Many of its leaders and intellectuals do not believe what the Catholic Church believes. And because of that, they do not teach what the Catholic Church teaches. […] Catholicism is dying in the German-speaking world, not because the gospel has been proclaimed and found incredible or hard, but because it hasn't been proclaimed with joy, confidence, and zeal. […] Recognizing that hard truth is the only path toward a German Catholicism that has something credible to say to the rest of the world Church.' George Weigel, What kind of believers (09.10.2019): https://www.firstthings.com/web-exclusives/2019/10/what-kind-of-believers [18.08.2020]. In 2015 Weigel had already talked about 'The Catholic Church's German Crisis'. (https://www.firstthings.com/web-exclusives/2015/05/the-catholic-churchs-german-crisis. Such increasingly harsh polemics and accusations of heresy and schism show how important synodal processes such as the German one are if polarisation is not to get out of control, as it is in US society and Church.

6. See the description and theological analysis of the Central European synods: Wilhelm Rees and Ludger Müller (ed.), *Synodale Prozesse in der katholischen Kirche*, Innsbruck, 2016; Wilhelm Rees and Joachim Schmiedl (ed.), *Unverbindliche Beratung oder kollegiale Steuerung? Kirchenrechtliche Überlegungen zu synodalen Vorgängen.* Freiburg i.Br, 2016; Joachim Schmiedl/Robert Walz (Hg.), *Die Kirchenbilder der Synoden. Zur Umsetzung konziliarer Ekklesiologie in teilkirchlichen Strukturen*, Freiburg im Breisgau, 2015.

7. See *Gemeinsame Synode der Bistümer der Bundesrepublik Deutschland: Offizielle Gesamtausgabe*. Mit einem Vorwort von Karl Lehmann, Freiburg im Breisgau, 2016; Reinhard Feiter and Richard Hartmann/Joachim Schmiedl (ed.), *Die Würzburger Synode. Die Texte neu gelesen*, Freiburg im Breisgau, 2013. The texts of the Würzburg and Dresden synods are accessible online at: https://www.dbk-shop.de/de/Deutsche-Bischofskonferenz/Synodentexte.html [Accessed 09/02/2021].

8. See Eberhard Prause, 'Kirche hinterm eisernen Vorhang in Bewegung', in: Schmiedl and Walz (ed.), *Die Kirchenbilder*, pp 110–122.

9. See especially paras 6-8 of the Pope's letter and *Evangelii Gaudium* 11–13, 27–39.

10.Preparatory Forum 'Power and the Distribution of Power in the Church', Common Participation and Sharing in the Task of Mission, Paper for Synod Members S20 (Working Paper for the Session of the expanded Common Conference on 13/14 September 2019 in Fulda: https://www.synodalerweg.de/fileadmin/Synodalerweg/Dokumente_Reden_Beitraege/SW-Vorlage-Forum-I.pdf [Accessed 10/02/2021]

Synodality: Critical Questions and Gender Concerns from Asia

KOCHURANI ABRAHAM

The 'path of synodality' identified by Pope Francis as what "God expects of the Church of the third millennium" is a very attractive notion, yet confusing from the standpoint of those excluded from the clericalized leadership structures of the Catholic ecclesiastical life. This problematic is critically analysed from an Asian/Indian woman's perspective, bringing to relief gender concerns underlying the process of becoming a synodal church. The Indian Christian Women's Movement (ICWM), which is an autonomous platform that brings together women from the Christian denominations in India is presented as a model of synodality in praxis, a new way of being Church.

Many women and gender non-conforming persons dream of a Church where they have equal opportunities to share responsibilities of leadership and ministry in partnership with men at all levels. For them, the 'path of synodality' identified by Pope Francis as what "God expects of the Church of the third millennium" is very inviting yet baffling. The dilemma results from the fact that women and others who do not fit into the gendered hierarchy of the ecclesiastical system are at a loss to comprehend how they would step into making the synodal path unfold. This is because the significance and the practical implications of this splendid concept will be spelt out mainly by bishops who are all men and who have been enjoying the privilege of governing the Church. The rest of the ecclesiastical population comprising of women and other sexual minority groups do not have much of a say in articulating how they would like to see synodality happening in the Church at the different levels of ecclesiastical functioning though a token representation would be consulted. This being the case, the gender question in relation to a synodal Church coming into being, is a matter of serious concern that calls for critical interrogation at the level of theorizing and in praxis.

'Synodality' is an attractive notion as it implies sharing of power particularly when set against the backdrop of the prominent hierarchical structuring of the Church. However, the mode of becoming a synodal Church is perceived very differently by people depending on their positioning on the ecclesiastical pyramid. Power and space are intrinsically connected. Social space is not merely an arena in which power relations happen, but also one of the means with which power is sought to be exercised, observe social theorists.[1] For those who exercise leadership roles in the Church, synodality could mean power sharing in a top-down approach, whereby its terms and conditions are defined by those who hold ecclesiastical authority. Even if synodality indicates "the path along which the People of God walk together" – as pointed out by the International Theological Commission – this is something illusive for those occupying the bottom rungs of the hierarchical ladder or excluded totally from it. Since the clericalized hierarchy holds the reins of decision-making power in the Church, synodality cannot happen if the Christian faithful remain merely an 'obedient flock' though their voices may find a hearing during the formal synodal gatherings.

For synodality to become the way of being Church, it is imperative to bridge the clergy-'laity' divide. Here, language is indicative of the basic problematic underlying the issue. The term 'lay' denotes ordinary people, the non-experts as distinct from professionals or experts, who in the matters of faith are the clergy. If the baptized have to come of age as responsible members of the Church, there is a need for revisiting the ecclesiastical structures and related concerns that are instrumental in keeping Christian faithful infantile in matters of faith. While religious power is vested in the hands of the clergy and the majority of the baptized remain 'lay people', the path of synodality is starting on a wrong premise that could impede the aspirations of becoming a synodal Church.

Since the path of synodality envisions the Church as a community that journeys together, some questions arise in my mind as an Asian woman. In which way, will the notion of a 'Synodal Church' pave the way for women and others to walk together with men or, will it be another attempt to pour the 'new wine' into 'old wineskins' without the possibility of bringing about any systemic changes in the hierarchical structuring of ecclesiastical establishment? What is the freshness brought into the concept of synodality by Pope Francis that it can give an innovative impetus to new ways of being Church in the third millennium? While the 'upside-down pyramid' imagery is apparently promising in terms of subverting the possibilities of domination intrinsic to the normal pyramid structure, will it enhance the 'Ecclesiastical Quotient' of the faithful or is it merely an imagery that brings into relief the servant leadership of those who occupy positions of authority in the Church?

My primary concern is to bring in the voices of the marginalized/ excluded into this discourse on the synodal Church. However, we shall see first how synodality is perceived in the Asian/Indian context by the ecclesiastical leadership and then explicate how women with feminist theological sensibilities are initiating synodal practices from below, which give expression to new ways of being Church.

I Synodality in the Asian/ Indian Setting and Emerging Questions

In the Asian/Indian context synodality is generally understood and practiced as coming together of bishops at regular intervals to which representatives of laity would be invited depending on the themes that are deliberated. Even as synodal practices are perceived in the conventional sense, the notion of synodality is apparently very appealing to the Asian Churches as they see it as essential to ecclesiastical growth in a context as that of Asia which is culturally different from the West. This was made evident in a special proposal to the Holy See by the Japanese Church at the time of preparation for the Asian Synod in 1997. *The Japanese bishops asked the Holy See "to consider a system of establishing relationships not based on centralization but on collegiality" and "to give more recognition to the rightful autonomy of the Local Churches."*[2] In other words, synodality was seen as necessary to better inculturate the faith in the Asian context, which meant to «put on Asian clothes".[3] Since liturgical translations have been micromanaged by the Vatican, Asian Episcopal conferences have called for greater authority on this issue. In this context, they argue that Church reform requires decentralization, synodality.[4]

In the Indian ecclesiastical setting, since India is home to three Catholic rites, the possibilities of greater collegiality embedded into synodality are seen as a means of sorting out issues between the three rites of the Church in India. As opined by Bishop Thattil, "All the three Churches in India should work in a more synodal and collegial way."[5] Against the backdrop of the complex socio-economic and religio-cultural reality and the consequent challenges in the current political setting of India, the synodal ecclesiology of Pope Francis focusing on decentralization, participation and communion is seen as very pertinent for facilitating the contextual identity and growth of the Indian Church today.

Even as the hierarchy of the of the Asian/Indian setting finds synodality an engaging notion on the grounds that it would enable them to have greater powers to manage the ecclesiastical affairs of their particular contexts, an issue that is still shrouded in ambiguity is the question of the participation of women and other faithful in the affairs of the Church. The gender question gains currency before the discrepancies in the official Church's positioning in its claims to become a '*syn-hodos*' Church and the incapacity to re-frame its ecclesiology and ecclesiastical structures that will facilitate this process of becoming one. The exclusive male clerical leadership structure of the Church is a case in point here. Unless women also take active part in the life and mission of the Church and particularly in the decision-making process as noted by S. Karambi, the Church cannot be described as an organic communion and participatory in nature.[6]

At a press briefing on the Amazon Synod, when questions were raised about the contributions that women can offer**,** Cardinal Gracias, the president of the Catholic Bishops Conference of India asserts that neither Church law nor theology prohibit women from participating in active ways in the Church. All the same, he acknowledges that despite the decentralization urged by Pope Francis, bishops are not using the opportunities they have to involve women more. [7]

The contradictions underlying the gender question in the Church reminds me of a conversation that I had with a Catholic college professor some time ago. He spoke gloriously about women's empowerment and asserted that it should begin in the family. In his opinion, women and men are like two wheels of a car that should move together to sustain the growth and wellbeing of the family. However, when he was asked as to who made decisions in his family, he replied without a second thought that the car needs a driver and God has entrusted him with that responsibility since he was the 'head' of the family. Further, he substantiated his position by citing many biblical texts that supported his argument about his 'divinely ordained' role as the head. On the synodality question in the Catholic Church, I see a strong parallelism in the allegory of the 'wheels' and 'driver' imagery in family life and in ecclesial life.

The crucial question in this context is if the Christian faithful or the leaders of the Church consider baptism as the core sacrament that makes a person responsible for the Church's life and mission. If baptism is the defining factor, then it is important that the faithful wake up to a sense of being Church, what I term as the 'Ecclesiastical Quotient' and this calls for a process of enabling their capacity to exercise spiritual and theological leadership without the clerical tag. Unless and until the faithful are trained to assume ecclesiastical responsibility, the power of their baptismal grace could remain dormant. Delinking priestly ordination and jurisdiction becomes necessary if the faithful are to be awakened to their baptismal potential, and this would have a remarkable impact in the making of a synodal Church.

While listening to all the members of the Church is presented as the key to synodal life, the question arises as to who is the subject of this 'listening?' Even as the document on Synodality points to everyone in the Church as a subject, a "single communitarian subject,"[8] as long as the responsibility to listen and arrive at decisions rests exclusively in the hands of the male clericalized hierarchy, the ecclesiastical system will continue as of now with men driving the car while women and other non-clerical faithful remaining its wheels. The crisis of clergy sexual abuse and the incapacity of the all-male clerical leadership to deal with it effectively is an instance that signal to the urgency of including women and others in ecclesiastical leadership positions if synodality has to become the way of being Church in the third millennium.

The synodal path will pave the way for an *ecclesiogenesis,* when a new way of being Church evolves from the old.[9] This would happen when spiritual power is shared by all people, and people with spiritual agency irrespective of their gender or sexual orientation stand a chance to exercise leadership in the Church. Then the ecclesiastical polity will have to be democratic, where persons imbued with wisdom of the Spirit and the necessary leadership qualities are elected from the community of the faithful and they will be accountable to the community for the responsibilities they shoulder. When Church leadership emerges from the Christian faithful, from below, not hierarchically from above, synodality will become a lived experience in ecclesial life.

II Synodality in Praxis: Indian Women Birthing the Church Anew

For women who believe that they are Church and want to live their baptismal commitment to the full, the notion of synodality is apparently incompatible with the highly clericalized hierarchical system of exercising authority in the institutional Church. Being alienated from the leadership mechanisms of the Church, they find themselves incapacitated within their ecclesiastical framework to respond effectively to the new challenges of mission. This has led to the emergence of new synodal practices from below. In India, the praxis of synodality has found expression in the birthing of the Indian Christian Women's Movement (ICWM), which has brought together women from the different Christian denominations on a common platform to walk and discern together the path of living their baptismal commitment with greater intensity. For Indian Christian women, the initiation of ICWM in 2014 has been a conscious and concrete move on their part 'to be the change'[10] they wish to see happening as Church today.[11]

Certainly, it is pertinent to ask why a movement like ICWM is needed in today's India. Generally speaking, Indian women are making rapid advancements in the socio-political and economic fronts, thanks to their changing consciousness in response to the increasing opportunities available to them. Yet, in spite of the many progressive developments in the secular sphere, the regressive traditions which persist in the garb of religion continue to have a say on Indian women's psyche. Against this backdrop, a movement like ICWM has become a decisive move to address the hegemonic hold of religion on women's lives.

In the context of a country like India where the patriarchal plot of 'divide and rule' thrives mainly on account of women's religious conditioning, Christian women coming together on an egalitarian platform in view of living their baptismal commitment with greater freedom is a major step. The Christian Churches in India are not homogeneous on the issue of women's participation in their particular churches and gender equality remains a distant dream since leadership continues to be a male domain. The Indian Christian Women's Movement has enabled Christian women to join hands with prophetic courage for addressing justice concerns in the Churches and in society.

The restlessness for justice that the members of ICWM share to is not limited to the ecclesiastical confines but there is a shared commitment to work towards an inclusive social order founded on egalitarian principles in the Indian society. Taking justice and liberation as Gospel imperatives, Christian women forge coalitions with people of goodwill who share this commitment and thus participate in discerning and living the Christian mission effectively. The movement also has members who belong to the LGBTQI groups and the criterion for membership or leadership is not their sexual identity or sexual orientation but their willingness to live their baptismal commitment with enthusiasm and responsibility.

As in the early Church community, persons endowed with wisdom of the Spirit-Sophia are elected to lead the movement at the national and regional levels. We believe as noted by Ruether that "a democratic polity better expresses the theological meaning of the Church as a redemptive society",[12] and so the movement engages in democratic processes, which makes synodality a lived experience. In this task, Mary Magdalene, the woman who has been rightly called 'the apostle to the apostles' is taken as the model of liberative leadership. For Indian Christian women who are emerging out of the gendered moulds in which they have been cast, Mary Magdalene is an icon of Christian discipleship who teaches them to embrace the newness of the Gospel and to be committed to realizing the vision of the reign of God. ICWM members find themselves challenged to be like her in accompanying those who are crucified today by unjust systems of power and to proclaim the resurrection that overcomes the forces of death. Thus, Mary's apostolic leadership becomes the key to ecclesiastical re-imagination as women are enabled to exercise their spiritual and theological agency in realizing a new social, religious and political order.

ICWM is not about creating an independent Church that runs parallel to the institutional ecclesiastical establishment. Members of ICWM continue to remain in full affiliation to the particular Churches to which they belong through baptism. However, ICWM becomes a space that enables Christian women to exercise their Christian discipleship in a manner that affirms their full humanity beyond patriarchal dictates. As a sisterhood of solidarity, ICWM becomes a base to challenge unjust beliefs, practices and structures that perpetuate oppressive ideologies and accentuate the exploitation of women and other marginalized sections of the Indian society. By raising questions of gender justice, it affirms the richness women can bring to their Churches if they can be modelled on the foundation of equal partnership in the different aspects of ministry and mission. It is a way of affirming that 'Women's Lives Matter' and women's contributions are intrinsic to the growth and well-being of any organization in the secular on religious sphere in any given society. Taking 'discipleship of equals' as the basis of ecclesial life, ICWM engages in subverting social hierarchies in order to give a new meaning to inclusion and belongingness. In doing so, Christian women are enabled to tackle the gendered politics of inclusion/exclusion as prevalent in their Churches and in society.

ICWM takes ministry as the praxis of the Reign of God as observed by Schillebeeckx. Subsequently, if New Testament ministries did not form or develop from and around the Eucharist but from the formation of the community as Schillebeeckx argues, leadership and structures of the community need to emerge on the basis of the gift of the Spirit, from which no one is excluded.[13] This calls for the creative transformation of the Church structures with new forms of participation, communication, diaconal action and Church leadership.[14] On this key, ICWM becomes a new way of being Church where women journey together with people of goodwill and thus translate to life the path of synodality at the service of the Reign of God.

To conclude, in my thinking, the notion of synodality has far more wider and deeper implications than assemblies of bishops however consultative and participative they may be. It is not to be limited to an ecclesiastical stretching from a euro-centric Church to greater expressions of autonomy for local Churches. These moves would only lead to cosmetic changes in the way of being Church if the male clericalized hierarchy continues to the axis of global Catholicism.

In the idea of a 'Synodal Church', I hear the stirring of the Spirit calling the Church to return to its founding vision and character, as a community modeled after the path tread by Jesus Christ in initiating the Reign of God in this world. It can be a 'turning point' in the evolutionary story of the Church, when it paves the way for the Church to become freed of its feudalistic, imperialistic and patriarchal baggage and the structures ensuing from these historical conditioning. For this to happen, it is necessary to critically revisit the trajectory of the development of ecclesiastical structures of leadership that have evolved in the context of particular socio-political situations and rethink the clericalized, gendered and hierarchical ecclesiological traditions that sustain them. 'Synodality' will become a re-birthing and revitalizing path for the Church when baptismal commitment and not priestly ordination becomes the crux of ecclesial life and Christian faithful learn to take responsibility for ecclesiastical life and mission. This will enable the emergence synodal Church in a manner that translates to life the Gospel politics of Jesus Christ.

Notes

1. Satish Deshpande, "Hegemonic Spatial Strategies: The Nation-Space and Hindu Communalism in Twentieth century India" in Partha Chattergee and Pradeep Jaganathan (eds), *Community, Gender and Violence,* Subaltern Studies XI, New Delhi: Permanent Black, 2000, 167-211.
2. Catholic Bishops' Conference of Japan, "Special Assembly for Asia of the Synod of Bishops: Official Response of the Japanese Church to the Lineamenta," July 23, 1997, at https://www.cbcj.catholic.jp/1997/07/23/5384/ [20 July, 2020].
3. Thomas C.Fox, "From the Synod for Asia," May 4,1998, at http://natcath.org/NCR_Online/documents/synod1.htm [20 July 2020].
4. Thomas Reese citing Cardinal Oswald Gracias, "Church reform requires decentralization, synodality," National Catholic Reporter, Feb 11, 2016, at https://www.ncronline.org/blogs/faith-and-justice/church-reform-requires-decentralization-synodality [22 July 2020].
5. Bp Raphael Thattil, "Three Churches in India Work in a More Synodal Way", Light of Truth, 15 October, 2018, at http://lightoftruth.in/coverstory/three-churches-india-work-synodal-way/ [30 July 2020]

6. Karambai S. Sebastian, "Participation of the laity in the decision-making structures of the local church," at http://www.canonlawsocietyofindia.org/research/participation-of-the-laity-in-the-dicision-making-structures-of-the-local-church/ [2 August, 2020].
7. Vatican News, 'Amazon Synod Briefing: Role of women, Inculturation, Synodality' at https://www.vaticannews.va/en/vatican-city/news/2019-10/amazon-synod-briefing-role-of-women-inculturation-synodality.html, [30 July 2020].
8. International Theological Commission, Synodality in the Life and Mission of the Church, no.55
9. Leonardo Boff introduced the term *ecclesiogensis* to show how a new way of being Church emerges from the basic Christian communities in the Latin American context. See Leonardo Boff, *Ecclesiogenesis*: *The Base Communities Reinvent the Church,* Maryknoll NY: Orbis Books, 1986.
10. "Be the change you wish to see in the world" is a saying attributed to Mahatma Gandhi.
11. The idea of initiating ICWM emerged at the National Women's Conference on "Paradigm Shifts in Vatican II and its Impact on Women" co-organized by Streevani (a feminist Catholic NGO, Pune, India) and a few other Catholic organizations at Bangalore from 8 to 11 January, 2014. The presence of an ecumenical sister as a resource person, who voiced the need for Christian Women to join hands in their fight for gender justice in the Churches found a strong echo among the participants and this led to the birthing of the Indian Christian Women's Movement (ICWM).
12. Eugene C. Bianchi, Rosemary Radford Ruether, *A Democratic Catholic Church: The Reconstruction of Roman Catholicism*, NY, Crossroad, 1992, 206.
13. Sehillebeeekx, Edward: *Ministry: Leadership in the community of Jesus Christ,* New York, Crossroad, 1982.
14. Hermann Haring, "The Authority of Women and the Future of the Church" in Elisabeth Schussler Fiorenza and Hermann Haring (ed) The Non-Ordination of Women and the Politics of Power", *Concilium,* 1993/3, 117-125.

The Amazon Synod: Synodality as a Meeting Place for Diversity

AGENOR BRIGHENTI

With the Amazon Synod as a starting point, an approach to synodality is being developed that considers the relationships of local to global, that is to say the concept of universality as the convergence of diverse characteristics. As a new topic and paradigm, the Amazon transcends the Amazon, conferring a planetary reach on the regional synod. As a consequence of the Amazon Synod, the periphery that came to its heart, provoking instability and fear, the Church is being challenged to move away from its internal focus so it can embrace the interpellations of the Spirit which, in today's Church, come above all from the southern hemisphere.

I Introduction

The Amazon Synod, the launch of a new approach for this advisory body to the Primate[1], brought the periphery into the heart of the Church, provoking instability and fear particularly within certain areas of the Roman Curia. Its regional nature, given that the Amazon resonates beyond "the Amazon", far from confining it to its local context and being nothing more than the expression of its Churches requirements, constituted an exercise of synodality expressed through the relationship of local to global. Universality, as a convergence of individual diversity, differs fundamentally from universal generalisations, from traits with pretensions to universality that impose themselves on others through approaches that are typical of colonialism in both thought and practice.

The Latin American Church has a long standing practical experience of synodality, above all through the implementation of conciliation and renewal, although not without misunderstandings and obstacles, principally to be found in the dominant centre, feeling itself unsettled by the periphery. Nevertheless, the learnings and the legacy of the Latin American Bishops five General Conferences of an Ecclesio-Genesis Church embodied in the communion of small "Base Communities", as well as the exercise of shared planning with decision making through inclusive bodies such as councils and pastoral assemblies, consolidated a Church of "communion and participation" that not even the three decades of "ecclesial involution"[2] prevailing during the two previous pontificates, succeeded in neutralising.[3] To the extent that the Amazon Synod not only succeeded in the reaffirmation of conciliar renewal and the ecclesiastic liberational tradition but also set forward bold proposals for addressing its needs. In a world that is increasingly diverse and pluralistic and finding itself in the midst of a whole range of fundamentalists, traditionalists and authoritarians, the Church, just as the Amazon Synod predicated, needs to bear witness to the communion of those who are different and to welcome their differences in the defence and promotion of the lives and ecosystems of the poor.

I Universality and universalism

The emergence of a planetary conscience which sees in the multifaceted map of sensitivity to the ecological crisis, the interdependence of markets, of techno-science – particularly robotics and data - as much as to military strategy, politics and spirituality, brings a note of continuous tension to the debate about the relationships of global to local and the particular to the universal. A tension that made itself felt equally in the Amazon Synod in the inter-relationships of the local Churches with some parts of the universal Church.

a) The Amazon Synod; a regional synod?

The convocation of the Amazon Synod by Pope Francis, both in its preparation and delivery and, now, in its implementation, created tensions and even opposition from both within and outside the Church.[4]

A first objection to the Synod came from those who argued that

Amazonia was a local reality, while the Bishops' Synod was universal, as if the Amazonian biomass constituted a reality that was separate from the countries of which it was a part, from the continent and from the planet. From the ecological point of view, far beyond the nine countries over which it extends, its devastation is already creating serious consequences for all humanity. From an ecclesiastical standpoint, both the ecological question and the fragile presence of the Church in this region, that is crying out for help, impact on all Churches' duties of care in a shared responsibility for evangelical action.

A second objection to the Synod argued that ecology was a problem for environmentalists and inappropriate as an agenda item for the Church. This ignores the fact that, as part of biblical revelation from Genesis to the Apocalypse, the vocation of being human as a co-creating creature, calls us to be a guardian of Creation, to care for our Shared Home. It appears that they are unaware of the fact that the issue of ecology, above all in recent decades, has occupied an important place within Church social doctrine, both in the teachings of John Paul II and Benedict XVI and particularly in those of Pope Francis who dedicated an encyclical exclusively to this issue (*Laudato Si*), highlighting the concept of "integral ecology" joining "the cry of the earth with the cry of the poor" (L.Boff).

A third objection to the Amazon Synod consisted in the insistence that the indigenous Amazonian tribes needed to be evangelised just like everyone else, and, as such, needed to be integrated within modern western society, as if evangelisation did not imply the incorporation of the Gospel within cultures and that these needed to be respected and protected. Or, as if the indigenous tribes, unlike any and every other group of people, were not entitled to their own identity, to their right of self determination, to preserve the right to their historical cultural and religious roots.

b) Between local and global

The three objections against the Amazon Synod have various underlying issues. One of them is ecclesiological, particularly where the Church strives to be catholic and universal. For K. Rahner, the main change arising from Vatican II was to place catholicity within the Local Church, quite the opposite of that was envisaged by the previously prevailing ecclesiology. This defended the existence of a Universal Church, which both preceded and manifested itself within the Local Churches (the dioceses) and of which the Pope was both the representative and the guarantor. These Local Churches would be "portions" of the Universal Church and, in consequence, the bishops would be collaborators of the Pope - the bishop of all bishops. The ecclesiology of Vatican II, however, in going back to the biblical and patriarchal roots positioned the catholicity of the Church within each Local Church, in communion with the other Churches. It affirmed that there was no Church that either preceded or stood outside the Local Churches. The Diocese is a "portion" of God's people and not a "part" (a portion contains something of everything). Within each Local Church, a depository of the totality of the mystery of salvation, would be found the "Church in its entirety", even though in itself it did not constitute the "entire Church", given that none of them alone could fully fathom this mystery.

For W. Kasper, and in light of Vatican II, the notion of a Universal Church that both preceded and manifested itself within the Local Churches and of which the Pope was the representative and guarantor is an "ecclesiological fiction". Any such universality would go no further than being the expansion and imposition of one key characteristic over others and, furthermore, of a universalism within a framework of asymmetric, vertical, domineering and colonial relationships. The 'one" Church is a "Church made up of Churches"[5], presided over by the Bishop of Rome, each combining autonomy and communion with the other Churches. In this nascent Church, each Local Church takes its own shape, not as a subsidiary nor as a copy of a supposed "Mother Church", but each in its different ways, with its own countenance, a new culture with common characteristics[6]. Universalism, on the one hand, creates volatility at the local level, and on the other, expands and imposes one characteristic over others, making the Local Churches either copies or reflections of the supposed "Universal Church" which, in all reality, represents an extension of the characteristics of Rome[7]. Within universalism, there is an inherent dialectical relationship between global and local that pivots at the local level, with an implicit threat for the latter that the true sense of reality becomes volatile. However, with a move away from this true sense, there is a descent into generalities and unique characteristics are lost to sight. It is important to think both globally and locally, just as with any action that impacts at both global and local levels requiring system wide interventions simultaneously articulated globally and locally, with the local level as the starting point.

II Amazonia transcends Amazonia

It does this for two main reasons: because it springs forth as a new entity, staking its claim as a new interlocutor crying out for respect, care, support and appreciation; and, also, because it establishes itself as a new paradigm calling for new ways of looking at life and its surroundings and for new patterns of relationships with others, with nature and with the transcendent.

a) Amazonia as a new being

From both the social and ecclesiastic perspectives, Amazonia bursts forth as a new kind of entity, in the first place because of the *ecological question*, which predicates nature as a subject matter for the law, indeed with jurisprudence already existing in some countries. Contrary to the stance taken by the ultra new liberals, a concern for nature is not a left wing ideology, invented by communists against capitalism and progress. Nature is not just the "environment" but something that shapes the whole, within which "everything is interconnected"; there is a chain of life, an interdependence of living things. We are not simply on the earth, we are the earth. Let us not forget Pope Francis' words that every creature, "has its own intrinsic value"[8].

And in the second place, Amazonia springs forth as a new kind of entity because the tribes whose origins are there argue for their just entitlements to territory, culture, value systems and ways of life. The world is increasingly diverse and challenges us all not only to live along side those who are different, but also to learn how to enrich ourselves through those differences. Seeking to defend their existence, their identity and to preserve their values and traditions there are more than a hundred tribes in Amazonia who are in "voluntary isolation". Yet, those who today are in isolation, tomorrow will be open to living convivially with other peoples and cultures, provided that a symmetrical relationship can be established based on dialogue and equality, distinct from all and any colonially based approach.

b) Amazonia as a new paradigm

From the Amazonian ecology and "tribes of the rainforest" apart from the appearance of new citizens, there is also the emergence off a new paradigm that needs to be taken into account as much in the social context as the ecclesiastical[9]. From an ecological standpoint, viewing the "other" side, the natural world, from a position of dominance, leads to predatory and destructive ways of approaching things. However, when this is seen as an integral part of self and as a gift from God, it becomes something to be admired and cared for, a respectful relationship and responsibility, a mediation of God. The suggestive title of the Synod's Final Exhortation – *Querida Amazônia* – establishes an affectionate and loving relationship with nature. The Pope tells us, "we need to learn from the indigenous tribes to become fully aware of Amazonia, to love and not simply exploit it; and, in doing this, we can feel intimately linked to it such that Amazonia becomes part of us, like a mother".[10]

Amazonia appears as a new paradigm from the ethnic point of view, as it challenges the view of the "other" in so far as the tribes living in the region are concerned not as people that are backward and savage, getting in the way of the expansion of the frontiers of agriculture and mining, but as a race that is different with its own civilisation, values, as subjects with the same rights as all humankind, starting with the right to be themselves and live in their homelands. This implies overcoming any vestiges of colonial thinking and practice, historically epitomised by the drive for profit and violence. The Synod acknowledged that, even in evangelisation, "frequently, the sharing of the good news of Christ is done alongside those in power, who exploit natural resources and oppress their people".[11]

Assuming that the indigenous tribes are a paradigm within the context of evangelisation, means that we learn from and with them how to experience the blessings of a harmonious relationship between living things and with our Creator, in a measured and happy existence that the tribes have called – "the good life", in the Quechuan language – *sumak kawsay.*[12]

III When the periphery arrives at the heart of the Church

Pope Francis, hailing himself as coming from "the end of the world", has called on the Church "to get out to its edges without seeking to domesticate the frontiers".[13] The Latin American Church has a long tradition in the practice of synodality but, being at the periphery, has been in permanent tension with a universalistic and universalising centre. At Vatican II, those bishops from the subcontinent, while members of the Council, were not considered as a "territory" within the Council and so were not able to contribute as much, although subsequently considered to be its best "sons". When they returned home, they immediately set about using the Medellin Conference (1968) to hold a "creative reception" for the Council, transforming the Basic Ecclesiastic Community into an "initial cell for ecclesiastical restructuring".[14] They set themselves up in the natural setting for liberation theology, the first theology to be different from the one and only, centrally based theology and which came into being on the periphery. In spite of a plan of campaign that acted as a brake on the nascent liberation ecclesiology as designed in the CELAM Assembly in Sucre (1972), in what ensued from the Puebla Conference (1979), from Medellin and from Santo Domingo (1992)[15] to a point where it was stagnating, the Aparecida Conference (2007) and the election of the Pope (2013), restored the process of the renewal of the Council and its "creative reception", confirming the synodical trajectory of the Church in Latin America.

a) A new profile for the Bishops' Synod

The Bishops' Synod had its birth in the renovations of Vatican II as an expression of the commitment of the Local Churches to the activities of the Bishop of Rome's Primacy. However, while it was conceived as a group for deliberation, it became a consultative body and ended up being a forum that was more about information. Pope Francis decided to make it more synodical and effective. With this in mind, he promulgated the Apostolic Constitution *Episcopalis communio*[16] in September 2018 making the Synod, " a channel more shaped for evangelisation in today's world than to the self preservation" of the Church (n.1) as well as more intimately linked to the *sensus fidei* (sense of the faith) of all God's people, at the heart of which the Bishop, as well as a teacher, also becomes a "disciple who, knowing that the Spirit is granted to every one who is baptised, positions himself to listen to the voice of Christ, who talks through all of God's People" (n. 5). In consequence, the Synod needs to be less about being Bishops and, "become increasingly a privileged instrument for hearing the voice of God's People, also incorporating " people who do not hold the office of Bishop" (n.6). So "it will be increasingly apparent that within the Church of Christ there exists a deep communion between pastors and the faithful" (n.10).

Although modest, these are important changes. Modest because, while it has to become more deliberative given that the final document is official in character, women continue without a right to vote and experts without a right to have a say, limited to technical roles. On the other hand, however, in the case of the Amazonian Synod, being an expression of greater synodality, what stands out, *inter alia*, are: the broad and participative preparatory work, which mobilised Local Churches in the region as a whole; impressive numbers of God's People, particularly natives and women being an integral part of the assembly; all assembly members having an equal right to speak at any time[17]; the Pope being a constant member of the assembly, just like other members, taking part in discussions and voting with them; a right for the non-bishop members to take part in the votes: the final statement democratically voted on and the outcome made public; the Pope's Final Exhortation liked to the entire synodical process[18]; the finally document acquiring official status and not being substituted by the Final Exhortation.[19]

b) When the Spirit comes from the other direction

At the Amazon Synod, the periphery arrived at the centre creating instability, fear, reaction and opposition, mainly coming from certain parts of the Roman Curia. For them, used to being at the centre of things and to seeing the periphery from a vertical perspective, it went beyond the pale to be on the same platform as a "bishop from the rainforest", whom they saw as "little more than an indian with a mitre ", as a Paraguayan Bishop observed in the 1955 Rio de Janeiro Conference, confronted by the control from Rome. For them, it seemed a nonsense to be asked to listen to the Spirit though the voices of people that they generally held to be poorly evangelised, syncretic, pantheistic in their veneration of the *Pacha Mama* and with the audacity to come into St Peter's Basilica dressed in their traditional costumes and ornaments, to make an altar offering at Mass with the Pope presiding. Faced by comments ridiculing them at one of the General Congregations, Pope Francis inquired, "what is the difference between an indian headdress and the biretta worn by some officials at our Pontifical Council?" The Spirit blows where it wills, very frequently from unexpected quarters, along paths that can be attributed to God, but never serves as a projection of the "I" and is more likely to own the truth than be possessed by it.

IV In conclusion

The Amazon Synod, consistent with the needs and challenges that the region is facing, and based on a process of listening and consultation, was sufficiently bold to make some daring proposals. Given that it is not deliberative, since synodality continues to be muzzled by centralisation, particularly by the Roman Curia, the Pope, who in the present approach still retains the power decisions on certain matters, either chose not to make any pronouncements or, probably, was not allowed to decide. Given this, is synodality at an impasse? Would the Roman Curia, whose approach is fast reaching the end of its time, be willing to contemplate the much longed for "healthy decentralisation",[20] granting freedom to such bodies as the Episcopal Conferences or the recently created Ecclesial Conference of the Amazon (Conferência Eclesial da Amazônia) with the empowerment and autonomy to decide? Synodality, as an expression of the *sensus fidei* , needs its own channels and bodies to receive the interpellations of other Spirit that "blows where it wills" (John 3,8) universalising the convergence of diverse characteristics.

Translated by Christopher Lawrence

Notes

1. Cf. Cardeal Humes, Dom Claudio, *O Sínodo da Amazônia*, Ed. Paulinas: São Paulo, 2019.
2. Cf. González Faus. José Ignacio, "El meollo de la involución eclesial", *Razón y Fe* 220, nn.1089/90 (1989) p.67-84.
3. Cf. Libânio, João Batista, *A volta à grande disciplina: reflexão teológico-pastoral sobre a atual conjuntura das Igreja* (*Col. Teología e evangelizacão*, n.4), Ed. São Paulo: Loyola, 1984.
4. Cf. Grillo, Andrea, "As Igrejas ocidentais não devem apoderar-se do sínodo amazônico", 03 March 2020, in: http://www.ihu,unisinos.br/78-noticias/596733-as-igrejas-ocidentais-

nao-devem-apoderar-se-do-sinodo-amazonico-entrevista-com-andrea-grillo (accessed on 27 fev. 2020).
5. Cf. Tillard, Jean Marie Roger, *Église d'Églises. L'ecclésiologie de communion.* Paris; Les Éditions du Cerf, 1987.
6. França Miranda, Mario de, *Igreja Local, Atualidade Teológic*a 34(2010), p.40-58, here p.44. CF. Legrand, Henri, "la réalisation de l'Église en un lieu", in *Initiation à la pratique de le théologie*; vol. III, Cerf, Paris, 1993, p.1245s.
7. Lima Vaz, Henrique Cláudio de, "Igreja-reflexo vs Igreja-fonte", in *Cadernos Brasileiros*, n.46, abr.1968., p.17-22.
8. Papa Francisco, *Exortaçao Apostólica Pós-Sinodal - Querida Amazônia. Ao Povo de Deus e a todas as pessoas de boa vontade*, São Paulo: Paulinas, 2020, n.54.
9. Cf. Roca Alazar, Fernando, "El Sínodo amazônico, La Amazonía y la Iglesia", in *`Perspective Teológica,` Belo Horizonte*, v.51,n.1,Jan./Abr.2019, p.55-67.
10. Papa Francisco, *Querida Amazônia*, n.55.
11. Sínodo Pan-Amazônico, *Documento Final do Sínodo Pan-Amazônico*, in https:// www.ofm.org.br/ artigo/documento-final- do-sinodo-da-amazonia-28102019-081005 no.15[acesso em 12 nov.2019].
12. Cfg. Alcantara, Liliane Cristine Schlemer/Sampaio, Carlos Alberto Cioce, "Bem viver como paradigma de desenvolvimento: utopia ou alternativa possível?", in *Desenvolvimento e Meio Ambiente, Curitíba*, v. 40, abril 2017, p. 231-251.
13. Cf. Papa Francisco, "Entrevista a Antonio Spadaro", in *L'Osservatore `romano, edición semanal en lengua española, Año XLV*, no. 39 (2.333) Friday 27 of September, 2013.
14. CELAM, *Conclusões de Medellín. A Igreja na atual transformação da América Latina à luz do Concílio*, Petrópolis: Vozes, 1968, n. 15,10.
15. Cf. Keller, Miguel Angel, *El proceso evangelizador de la Iglesia en América Latina, De Río a Santo Domingo*, Instituto Pastoral de Celam, Medellín 1995, p.5-43.
16. Pope Francis, *Constitução Apostólica Episcopal. Sobre o Sínodo dos bispo.*s, Citá de Vaticano, 2018
17. Cf. Secretaria Generalis Synodi Episcoporum. *Regulamento Amazonia: nuovi cammini per la chiesa e per una ecologia integrale*, Citá del Vaticano, 2019.
18. Cf. Luciani, Rafael, Querido Amazónia: "O surgimento de uma 'nova hermenêutica'", in http://www.ihu.unisinos.br/78-noticias/596292-querida-amazonia-e-a-emergencia-de-uma-nova-hermeneutica-no-magisterio-artigo-de-rafael-luciani [Accessed on 27 February 2020].
19. Pope Francis justified approach saying, "The Exhortation Querida Amazônia neither replaces nor repeats the Final Document", since it is the product of the reflections of people who "know the Amazon's issues better than either I or the Roman Curia do, because they live there, and they suffer for it and love it passionately" (*Querida Amazônia*, n.3).
20. Pope Francis, *Exortação Apostólica Evangelii Gaudium. A alegria do Evangelho*, São Paulo: Paulinas, 2013, n.32.

Part Two: Biblical, Anthropological, and Practical Approach to the Reality of Synodal Life

Synodal and Collegial Thinking and Acting in the New Testament

BARBARA E. REID OP

There are numerous intimations of synodality and collegiality in the New Testament. In this essay, I first examine texts that show synodal ways of thinking and acting in the early Christian communities through their collective prayer, common meals, sharing of resources, and corporate engagement in the evangelizing mission. I then look for glimmers of collegiality in two episodes recounted in the Acts of the Apostles where threats to the harmony of the church were resolved by the leaders. Finally, I reflect on how new scientific understandings could shed light on dynamics of synodality in the church.

In the New Testament, there is a strong foundation for the current movement toward synodal and collegial ways of thinking and acting. In the document "Synodality in the Life and Mission of the Church" issued by the International Theological Commission in 2018,[1] synodality and collegiality are understood within an ecclesiology of communion, which emphasizes "the common dignity and mission of all the baptised, in exercising the variety and ordered richness of their charisms, their vocations and their ministries. . . . In this ecclesiological context, synodality is the specific *modus vivendi et operandi* of the Church, the People of God, which reveals and gives substance to her being as communion when all her members journey together, gather in assembly and take an active part in her evangelising mission" (§6). Collegiality is "the specific form in which ecclesial synodality is manifested and made real through the ministry of Bishops on the level of communion of the local Churches in a region, and on the level of communion of all the Churches in the universal Church" (§7). In this essay, I will examine first a sampling of New Testament texts that illustrate synodal ways of thinking and acting in the early Christian communities. I will then look for glimmers of collegiality in two episodes recounted in the Acts of the Apostles where leaders resolved threats to the harmony of the church. Finally, I reflect on how new scientific understandings could shed light on dynamics of synodality and pose questions for how that might play out in the church.

I Synodality: Together on the Way

The word "synod" combines the Greek preposition *syn*, "with" and the noun *hodos*, "way, path," yielding the meaning "together on the way." While the word "synod" itself does not occur in the New Testament, the concept of togetherness is represented most strongly. And in the Acts of the Apostles, followers of Jesus are called "those who belonged to the Way" (9:2; see also 18:25, 26; 19:9, 23; 24:14, 22). The "togetherness" of the disciples is sounded from the first chapters of Acts. For example, the eleven, the women followers from Galilee, and Jesus's mother and siblings (1:14) are "all together in one place" (2:1) when the Spirit is given them.

1.1 Togetherness in Common Prayer, Communal Meals, and Shared Possessions

Following Peter's Pentecost speech, Luke describes life among the believers:

> All who believed were together and had all things in common; they would sell their possessions and goods and distribute the proceeds to all, as any had need. Day by day, as they spent much time together in the temple, they broke bread at home and ate their food with glad and generous hearts, praising God and having the goodwill of all the people. And day by day the Lord added to their number those who were being saved. (Acts 2:44-47; similarly 4:32-37)

This passage names three practices that marked the togetherness of followers of the Way: collective daily prayer, communal meals, and sharing of monetary resources. While Luke's description is idealized, it still provides a roadmap that contemporary Christians can follow for synodal living.

We can see in other New Testament texts that each of these three practices posed challenges at times. Right after Luke asserts that "the whole group of those who believed were of one heart and soul, and no one claimed private ownership of any possessions, but everything they owned was held in common . . . for as many as owned lands or houses sold them and brought the proceeds of what was sold. They laid it at the apostles' feet, and it was distributed to each as any had need" (Acts 4:32, 34-35), there is the story of Ananias and Sapphira who withhold some of the proceeds of a sale of property. Their failure to relinquish all the proceeds is made even more serious by their lie to the community. This grave breech of oneness has deadly consequences (Acts 5:1-11).

That togetherness at table also posed challenges is evident in Paul's correspondence with the Corinthians. One difficulty at table surfaces when some members, whom Paul dubs "strong," thought it permissible to eat meat sacrificed to idols, while others, "the weak," were scandalized by this (1 Cor 8:1-13). Paul's advice is that although eating such meat is immaterial, the strong should forego it so as not to cause a stumbling block for the weak. There were also conflicts rooted in differences in social status. When the community in Corinth would "come together as a church" (1 Cor 11:18), the richer members would arrive earlier and be sated with food and drink while the poorer members went hungry (1 Cor 11:17-34). Paul excoriates those who "show contempt for the church of God and humiliate those who have nothing" (v. 22). His solution is "when you come together to eat, wait for one another" and if you are hungry, then eat at home (vv. 33-34).

A glimpse into the liturgical life of the Corinthians also shows that praying together is not always free of conflict. While scholars still debate what was the precise point of tension in 1 Cor 11:2-16, whether head coverings or hairstyles, it came to the surface when the women prayed and prophesied in the communal gathering. This community also seemed to have trouble exercising their gifts in an orderly manner in the liturgical assembly (1 Cor 14:1-40). It is notable that in both these instances, Paul has in view not only desired harmony within the Corinthian community, but communion with other local churches, asserting: "we have no such custom, nor do the churches of God" (11:16) and urges conformity with practices "in all the churches of the saints" (14:33b).

An image Paul uses with the Corinthian community to urge them toward synodal thinking and acting is that of the Body of Christ with all its various parts working together (1 Cor 12:12-31; similarly, Rom 12:4-8). He stresses the equal value of all the parts despite their variety and their differing functions. He underscores the vital necessity of each member for the smooth functioning of the body. He advises giving greater honour to the weaker members so there may be no dissension in the body. The whole body shares in both the sufferings and the joys of each member.[2]

1.2 Paul: Embodying Synodality Across Diverse Local Churches

In the texts above we have looked at a few select passages that point toward the communion that the first followers of Jesus experienced and strove for in their gatherings through their prayer, communal meals, and sharing of material possessions. In these examples, the focus is on how a particular local community, such as in Jerusalem or in Corinth, strove for harmonious oneness within their own church as they journeyed together on the Way. Efforts toward synodality across differing local churches can also be seen in Paul's missionary efforts and letters. He connects one church to another by including greetings, as for example, when he concludes his letter to the Romans "all the churches of Christ greet you" (16:16). One concrete way he linked disparate communities was when the believers in Jerusalem were in need and Paul solicits monetary support for them from the other churches (1 Cor 16:1–4; 2 Cor 8:1–9:15; Rom 15:14–32).

1.3 Journeying Together in the Evangelizing Mission

In the ITC document, another aspect of synodality is "when all her members journey together . . . and take an active part in her evangelising mission" (§6). The evangelist that most emphasizes journeying together is Luke. During the Galilean ministry, as Jesus travelled through cities and villages, the twelve along with Mary Magdalene, Joanna, Susanna, and many other women accompanied him and took and active part in the evangelizing mission (8:1-3). Although Luke casts men and women disciples in different roles, with the male apostles being sent out on evangelizing journeys (9:1-6; 10:1-12)[3] and female disciples financing the mission (8:3)[4] and exercising hospitality toward traveling apostles (e.g., Martha in Luke 10:38-42; Lydia in Acts 16), women followers are clearly present in what may have been day journeys throughout the Galilee (8:1-3). They are among all Jesus's acquaintances who followed him on the journey to Jerusalem and witnessed his death (23:49), saw his burial (23:55), and found the tomb empty (24:1-11).

While each Synoptic writer constructs his narrative with Jesus making one fateful journey from Galilee to Jerusalem, Luke's travel narrative is the longest (9:51-19:44). Much of the material in this section is uniquely Lukan and it is here that the majority of the parables and other teachings are found. What Luke conveys is that one comes to understand and be committed to Jesus in the course of journeying with him. This theme comes to a climax in the post-resurrection scene where they eyes of Cleopas and his companion are opened and their hearts are set on fire while the Risen One explains everything to them on the Way (Luke 24:13-35).

The texts we have looked at are only a few select passages that point toward synodality among the first followers of Jesus: a communion they experienced by journeying together with him, engaging in his evangelizing mission, and gathering to pray and eat together, while sharing their resources in common.

II Glimmers of Collegiality

The ITC document describes collegiality in terms of ecclesial synodality manifested "through the ministry of Bishops on the level of communion of the local Churches in a region, and on the level of communion of all the Churches in the universal Church" (§7). In New Testament times, the various ministries were still very fluid; there is no clear description or definition of any office in the New Testament. What we do have are lists of desired qualities in an *episcopos* (literally, "overseer," often translated "bishop") in texts such as 1 Tim 3:1-7 and Titus 1:7-9.[5] There are, however, numerous references to leaders in the emerging church. I would like to examine two episodes in the Acts of the Apostles in which we might say there were glimmers of collegiality as leaders faced threats to communal harmony and engaged collaboratively to resolve these.

2.1 Ministerial tensions between Hebrews and Hellenists in Jerusalem (Acts 6:1-7)

The first episode is set in Jerusalem, where the number of disciples was increasing and tensions between the Greek-speakers and the Hebrew-speakers arose (Acts 6:1-7). The former lodge a complaint that their widows are being neglected in the daily distribution (*tē diakonia tē kathēmerinē*). The twelve call together the whole community of the disciples and declare that it is not right for them to neglect the word of God in order to wait on tables (*diakonein trapezais*, v. 2). They propose that the "brothers" (*adelphoi,* rendered "friends" in NRSV) choose seven men of good standing for table ministry while the twelve reserve to themselves the ministry of the word (*diakonia tou logou*, v. 4). According to Luke, this pleased the whole community (v. 5). After the choices were made, they had the seven stand before the apostles (who in Luke are equated with the twelve), who prayed and laid their hands on them (v. 6). The episode concludes as it began, with the number of disciples increasing in Jerusalem.

In Luke's description of the process, there might have been the possibility of a collegial approach by the twelve, when their first step was to call together the whole community of disciples (v. 2). But it quickly becomes apparent that a hierarchical and unilateral mode of decision-making is in play. There is no evidence that the community of disciples had any input; the only voice they appear to have is to affirm the solution imposed by the twelve (v. 5).[6] Unlike the process in Acts 15 (see below), there is no listening to diverse perspectives, no discernment. The twelve dictate the solution. The men in the community[7] do have a role in implementing the decision. They choose the seven for the table ministry, who are ratified by the twelve. Luke asserts that the whole community was pleased (v. 5), but one wonders what the widows, who were at the centre of the dispute, thought and whether they were as pleased as the men with the solution.

2.2. Intimations of Collegiality Among Leaders of Diverse Churches (Acts 15)

In Acts 15 we have a different and much more serious conflict, involving all the churches, not simply one local community. As Luke tells it, Paul and Barnabas are in Antioch of Syria after a preaching tour through

Iconium, Lystra, Derbe, Pisida, Pamphylia, Perga, and Attalia. Certain individuals came up from Judea teaching that circumcision was necessary to be saved. After Paul and Barnabas "had no small dissension and debate with them" (15:2), they, along with several others, "were appointed to go to Jerusalem to discuss this question with the apostles and the elders" (15:2). They are sent on their way by the church, and in Jerusalem they are welcome by "the church and the apostles and the elders," where they report "all that God had done with them" (15:4). But they encounter there also some believers who espouse circumcision and keeping the whole law of Moses (v. 5).

In Jerusalem, the apostles and elders meet together to consider the matter (15:6). There is much debate (15:7); then Peter voices support for Barnabas and Paul's position (15:7-11), followed by further testimony from Barnabas and Paul (15:12). James, the leader of the Jerusalem community, then turns to the Scriptures, weaving together Jer 12:15; Amos 9:11-12; and Isa 45:21, to interpret the present situation, after which he pronounces a decision, invoking also the Holy Spirit (15:13-21). He settles the matter with a compromise: all that is required of Gentile believers is that they abstain "from things polluted by idols and from fornication and from whatever has been strangled and from blood" (15:20). The council concludes when the apostles and elders, "with the consent of the whole church" (15:22), choose Barsabbas and Silas to accompany Barnabas and Paul to deliver the decision both orally and by letter. The letter is addressed to "the brothers" (*adelphoi*) of Gentile origin in Antioch and Syria and Cilicia from the "brother apostles and elders" (*hoi apostoloi kai hoi presbyteroi adelphoi*, 15:23). It is most likely that Luke intends this communication to be between male leaders, not all the "believers" as the NRSV translation of *adelphoi* would imply. The episode concludes with the congregation in Antioch rejoicing as the letter is read to them (15:30-31).

The decision-making process in Acts 15 has some intimations of collegiality, as the apostles and elders listen to testimony from leaders who have diverse experiences and who hold divergent positions. They rely on the Scriptures and the Spirit to guide them and they find a compromise solution that pleases the community in Antioch.

III Synodality and Collegiality in Light of the New Science

While we have only examined a few select texts, we can see in the New Testament a basis for synodal and collegial thinking and acting. As we articulate more fully how these important dynamics could play out in the church today, it would serve us well to look not only to Scripture and tradition, but also to the wisdom emerging from contemporary studies on leadership that consider learnings from new science. Leadership theorists, such as Margaret Wheatley[8] invite us to shift away from a Newtonian mechanistic and materialistic view of the universe, where it was thought that studying the parts leads to understanding the whole, and consider the mindset of new science that focuses on wholism rather than parts and gives attention to relationship and connectedness of all creation. This approach would seem to resonate quite well with synodal thinking and acting. Leaders using such approaches focus on eliciting possibility, generosity, and the gifts of the whole group, valuing diversity and risking experimentation, rather than problem solving, fear, and retribution in a command and control model.[9] Building circles of friends and fostering networks of compassion is another approach to leadership that generates new ideas and new ways of responding to the mission.[10] Adapting these learnings to ecclesial efforts at collegiality prompts questions about whether there might not be wider involvement of the whole body when it comes to direction setting and decision making. Might our walking together be strengthened if non-episcopal members of the body have a voice that goes beyond consultation?

IV Conclusion: The Pattern of the Self-Emptying Christ

The togetherness that the church in New Testament times lived and strove for was cemented through common prayer, communal meals, sharing of material possessions, and a common engagement in the evangelizing mission. Oneness of mind and heart required then, as now, continual efforts of genuine listening to one another from a stance of respect for each member of the body and discernment of the leadings of the Spirit. One other essential stance for building up a harmonious church is expressed eloquently by Paul in his letter to the Philippians. By patterning our lives on the self-emptying that is modeled on Christ's life, who moved from life with God, to life with humanity, and then through death to new life

(Phil 2:6-11), and by looking not to only to one's own interests, but to the interests of others (Phil 2:4), so we can build up the church in synodality and collegiality.

Notes

1. For the full text, see International Theological Commission, "Synodality in the Life and Mission of the Church," March 2, 2018 at http://www.vatican.va/roman_curia/congregations/cfaith/cti_documents/rc_cti_20180302_sinodalita_en.html#_ednref50 [Accessed 11.1.20].
2. In the letters to the Colossians and the Ephesians, the same metaphor takes on a different meaning. Christ is no longer identified with the church itself, but is "head of the body, the church" (Col 1:18; similarly, Eph 5:23). In 1 Corinthians and Romans, the image evokes circularity, mutuality, interdependence, as the members with their various and equally important functions are joined together with and in Christ. In Colossians and Ephesians, Christ is over the body as head, giving the metaphor a hierarchical cast.
3. In Acts of the Apostles, Luke's second volume, Paul is the primary journeyer in the evangelizing mission.
4. The noun *hyparchontōn* in the phrase *ek tōn hyparchontōn autais,* "out of their resources," refers to monetary resources and the possessive pronoun *autais*, "their," is feminine, indicating that the money belongs to the women; it is not from the common purse.
5. For a succinct description of the evolution of the office of bishop, see R. Kevin Seasoltz," Bishop," in Carroll Stuhlmueller (ed.), The Collegeville Pastoral Dictionary of Biblical Theology, Collegeville: Liturgical Press, 1996, 85-87.
6. For further analysis of this text, see Barbara E. Reid, "The Power of the Widows and How to Suppress It (Acts 6.1-7)," in Amy-Jill Levine with Marianne Blickenstaff (eds.), A Feminist Companion to the Acts of the Apostles, FCNTEW 9, London; New York: T & T Clark, 2004, 71-88. I propose that the problem is that the widows of the Hellenists were being overlooked in the distribution of ministerial tasks, they were not on the receiving end of the *diakonia.* It is notable that v. 1 says only that the widows were being neglected in the "daily ministry," *tē diakonia tē kathēmerinē,* without specifying in what way. The NRSV renders *tē diakonia tē kathēmerinē* as "the daily distribution" and adds the phrase "of food," which is not in the text.
7. While the masculine plural *adelphoi*, can designate an inclusive group of "brothers and sisters," given Luke's proclivity for male leaders, it is likely here he means only the males. The NRSV renders *adelphoi* as "friends," which is not an accurate translation.
8. See, e.g., Margaret J. Wheatley, Leadership and the New Science. Discovering Order in a Chaotic World, 3d ed., San Francisco: Berrett-Koehler, 2006.
9. See, e.g., Peter Block, Community. The Structure of Belonging, San Francisco: Berrett-Koehler, 2008; Ronald Heifetz, Alexander Grashow, Marty Linsky, The Practice of Adaptive Leadership. Tools and Tactics for Changing Your Organization and the World, Cambridge: Cambridge Leadership Associates, 2009.
10. Donna Markham, Spiritlinking Leadership. Working through Resistance to Organizational Change, New York: Paulist, 1999.

The African Palaver Method: A Model Synodal Process for Today's Church

STAN CHU ILO

Many traditional African societies have a rich social and spiritual heritage. The African palaver is the art of conversation, dialogue, and consensus-building in both decision-making and in decision-taking in society. African Christians should recover and bring it to the table in the current search for local and universal approaches to resolving conflicts, and healing the polarisation in our churches on questions of faith and morals, and maintaining a dynamic balance between tradition and innovation in the crisis of modernity in today's Church. The African palaver offers a good model of how a non-Western civilization, long before the current conversation in the Church on synodality, developed practices of listening, engaging, dialoguing, and discerning the truth about things, and the path for the future. Traditional African societies created a sacred space for creative dialogue in communal decision-making, where everyone's voice, concerns and insights were welcomed. A variant of the African palaver is in the Igbo ethnic group of West Africa.

I What is the African Palaver?

"The African palaver (l'arbre à palabre) is a unique art of conversation and creative dialogue in the common search for practical solutions to everyday challenges and conflicts in personal, family, communal, and inter-communal relationships." What has been translated in the English language as "palaver" is a poor rendering of a rich ancestral socio-ethical religious tradition found in many African ethnic groups. This tradition provides the tools in the traditional setting for maintaining justice, peace, social cohesion, and for promoting those sound ethical choices which promote the common good and human and cosmic flourishing.

Among the Maasai of East Africa, palaver is what is designated by the tradition of *enkiguena*; and among the Zulu of Southern Africa, it is designated as *Indaba*. A short analysis of the roots of the cognate words for 'palaver' among the Igbo of West Africa will shed light on the profound meaning the art of conversation designated in the writings of many African scholars as *the African palaver*.

"The African palaver invites all people concerned in the community to a sacred space for creative dialogue" on how to promote those ethical norms which promote abundant life, and combat those vices or unjust acts which hamper the participation of all in the bond of life. Masamba ma Mpolo sees the African palaver as a gathering space for sharing the Word which gives life. Life is understood in this sense in many ways—a vital principle with an unbroken chain of being from God, and ancestors to humanity and all creatures; flourishing, being who one is meant to be; being in a right relationship, participating and contributing to the common good, and sharing in the common good. Life refers not only to the living (the gathered assembly), rather to the community—a rich and expansive notion which includes the living, the ancestors, the not-yet born, all spiritual realities, the visible and invisible creatures, ecological life, the planet and the entire cosmos. Everyone in the community has something to contribute to the shared bond of life. This is why Mpolo identifies the freedom and right to speak and the inclusiveness of the palaver community to hearing everyone's opinion as decisive. So, everyone is allowed to speak in their own manner, whether by words, dance, stories, symbols, and in mimes.

II Principles and Practices of the African Palaver among the Igbo of West Africa

> *ótù áká ànághị èké ńgwùgwù – One hand does not tie the parcel (you cannot clap with one hand)*

In his African classic, *Things Fall Apart*, set in pre-colonial Igboland in Eastern Nigeria, Chinua Achebe writes: "Among the Ibo the art of conversation is regarded very highly, and proverbs are the palm oil with which words are eaten. Okoye was a great talker and he spoke for a long time, skirting around the subject and then hitting it finally."[1] In this episode, Okoye had come to collect the debt which Unoka owed him. "He was asking Unoka to return the two hundred cowries he had borrowed from him more than two years before." But as soon as Unoka understood that the reason Okoye came to him that morning was to collect the debt he owed him, "He burst out laughing. He laughed loud and long and his voice rang out clear as the *ògénè,* and tears stood in his eyes. His visitor was amazed, and sat speechless."

Then Unoka began to speak, "Look at the wall...Look at those lines of chalk," and Okoye saw groups of the short perpendicular lines drawn in chalk. There were five groups, and the smallest group had ten lines. Unoka continued, "Each group there represents a debt to someone, and each stroke is one hundred cowries. You see, I owe that man a thousand cowries. But he has not come to wake me up in the morning for it. I shall pay you, but not today. Our elders say that the sun will shine on those who stand before it shines on those who kneel under them. I shall pay my big debts first." Okoye rolled his goatskin meant for sitting and departed.[2]

This episode ends without Okoye collecting his debt from a man who has been owing him for two years. Okoye also did not threaten to sue Unoka or call the bailiff. He understood the precarious financial difficulties facing Unoka and left in silence. This episode reveals very important aspects of the African palaver among the Igbo.

The first is the power of the spoken Word in dialogue and the need for everyone to tell their own stories—their hopes, dreams, pains, and fears. African traditional societies valued freedom of expression. Indeed, Mpolo argues strongly that the African traditional society created this inclusive space for dialogue because "everything revolves around the word, for to speak is to live, to recognize and to affirm the existence of the other person. To be speechless is to be naked, to be deprived of oneself. Loss of freedom to communicate and to transmit life biologically are synonymous with death. Speech is creative because it often engenders life."[3]

Given the importance of speech, truth-telling is of vital importance; and lies and falsehood are frowned against: "Ability to have recourse to speech and to assess the acts of life is therefore essential. God becomes flesh in human speech and acts. When it is a matter of blessing and reinforcing life, *mpova* (speech) becomes *Nzambi,* i.e. the human word becomes the word of God. It is word which brings peace, reconciliation, health, life, the word which re-establishes the equilibrium of the community when it is in danger of disintegration."[4]

The palaver is a space for truth-telling, because the truth heals, binds, and restores the community; the depths, diversity and ramifications of truth are found in the traditional African community through patient listening, and openness and attention to the spoken word—spoken in freedom. This is why, "The dynamic of palaver permitted free expression; it was possible to pour out one's heart, to give testimony or to analyse together a conflict which might endanger the existence, i.e. the life, of the community. The chief was obliged to listen to everything, even if this took a whole week.... Here we have the discourse of the people, the word which liberates."[5]

The palaver creates that space for listening. In the dialogue in question, both parties listen to each other. We notice the use of different communication tropes, proverbs, symbolisms, and gestures to convey the intended meaning and arrest people's attention. Gerald Adewole in his study of the use of proverbs in *Things Fall Apart* noted that "just as the roasted or boiled yams taste better or sweeter when eaten with palm oil, so is conversation sweeter and more edifying when laced with proverbs."[6] Proverbs, he maintains serve as 'essential rhetorical strategies, words of wisdom,' 'with striking aesthetic and thematic strengths.'[7] In the palaver under review, both Okoye and Unoka employ proverbs to imaginative effects, uniting history and narration in a rich way, condensing the past, present and the future through appeal to ancestral wisdom hidden in the proverbs, and compressing and unpacking serious truths and opposing perspectives with cogency and oratorical finesse. Both auditors are transported into regions of engagement where existential problems, and practical wisdom meet in a common recognition of each other's perspectives leading to a gradual movement to a consensus which is applied as practical solutions to the stream and pastiche of daily life.

Second, the African Palaver "is an ethic for consensus-building in the common and dynamic search for how to preserve, promote, and protect the common good from which all should draw as from a well pool. It is also a means for healing divisions and hurts and wounds inflicted on people". It proceeds from the acceptance of the inherited practice of traditional African communities that the resolution of moral or existential complexities is not achieved through stubborn attachment to a single viewpoint, or the narrow reduction of one's purvey to a preconceived idea or a limited horizon of meaning. The palaver is thus a depolarizing space for listening, conversation, and the fusion of individual subjective horizon in the ever-expansive and dynamic horizon of the communal wisdom of the ancestors in the search for justice and peace. The goal is not to shut anybody's opinion down or to drown individual perspectives, concerns and insight in certain pre-fabricated communal answers to existential questions or ultimate concerns. The palaver is in this sense a path to phronesis brought about in a critical, constructive and creative way in order to strengthen the bond of life in the community.

This is shown clearly in this dialogue between Unoka and Okoye. We see here that inter-personal conflicts are often resolved through dialogue in a respectful manner. This does not mean that people never resorted to unethical means for resolving conflicts of this kind, but we are concerned with the ancestral ideal which all was to aspire towards. We have many other instances in the novel where this approach to consensus building and resolution is present. An interesting example was the resolution of the case of domestic violence brought against Uzuwulu in chapter ten of the novel, where the body of ancestral jurors (all clad in masks), *égwúgwú* , resolved the matter not by retributive justice, but through a restorative approach with conditions set for both parties on how to live together in harmony and repair harms inflicted on the families. The palaver method aims at helping people "to avoid extreme positions, intolerant mindsets, and inelegant language of discourse which demean others, distort the truth or divide the community" and which is capable of destroying the communal life or the human future.

Finally, the palaver is an ethics of communal discourse applied in the search for harmony and concord in daily interactions. We see this again in this discussion between Unoka and Okoye, there is no dualistic polarity. The goal of the palaver is not about punitive justice, or for creating opposing camps or of winners and losers or for defending the interest of one person or a group over the other. The goal of the palaver is to restore right relationship and social cohesion. Uchendu captures this very well when he says in a dialogue in chapter 15 of *Things Fall Apart*, "there is no story that is not true. The world has no end."[8] What is needed is a balance of story; the ability to see the truth through another side of the coin; and an ability to listen to another's stories and enter into that story and avoid a closed narrative because "the world has no end." In the story, Unoka knows that he was wrong in not repaying his debt, but the ideal sought for in the palaver between him and Okoye was about finding a consensus which in this case was that Okoye needed to be more patient with him as he was facing a bigger mound of debts owed other people than Okoye.

II The African Palaver a Model of Synodality

One of the central impulses of the papacy of Francis is synodality as an ecclesial practice, process and mission. Synodality, in Pope Francis is a communal discernment in which we listen to God so that with God we can hear the cry of the people, and we listen to the cries of the people and the earth so that through them God's voice can be heard more clearly in the Church and the world is, in my thinking, a hermeneutical key for understanding the papacy of Francis.[9]

When we look at the roots of the word, 'palaver' in Igbo language, we are struck by the amazing resonance between the roots of 'synod' (walking together) and of cognate words for 'palaver' in the Igbo language, namely: (1) *a coming together of people held together* by a shared bond of life—ancestral ties for example. This coming together which occurs in multiple sites is what Pope Francis has consistently referred to as a culture of encounter. It is only by entering into each other's stories that we can see the rich depth of God's footprints in history; (2) *a process in the search* for the path which God opens to God's people; (3) *a commitment to listening to everyone* especially those suffering, the marginalized and the forgotten so that together the collective wisdom of the faith community is enriched by all, and the truth of God will become more evident and present to the community in responding to the challenges and opportunities of present times.

Many words that are used to designate the palaver tradition of traditional Igbo society reflect these three aspects of synodality. First, *ọgbákọ* like synods is *a summons and gathering together* of representatives to the ancestral grove or cradle for a consultative meeting at which important decisions are made. These sacred sites of dialogue are often designated as *iro, obodo* meaning a sacred inclusive gathering space for open dialogue carried out in truth, reverence, and respect. Everyone has a right to participate in this discussion or to bring up an issue or a case, and speak freely in the assembly when invited to do so.

Second, what takes place in such a space is a process of listening to the stories and perspectives of people in a patient and respectful manner designated by words like *ịgbá ìzù,* (to have an intimate discussion), *ịchịkọtá úchè ọnụ* (to deliberate and gather individual wisdom into a common consensus or common wisdom), *ịkpá ńkàtá* (an open narrative process of seeking for solutions to problems by exploring the vast array of ancestral wisdom mediated through the conversation partners). Each of these terms designate a process of discourse, debate, dialogue, and meeting of minds by individuals, family members, communities, and age groups, social organizations and women's group. The guiding operation for palaver among the Igbo people is *ìgwèbùíké* (a unity of perspectives and of efforts gives harmony and strength to the community in problem-solving).

Third, is the commitment of everyone to the search for truth and implementing what was decided upon. It is only through engagement with each other's stories can a collective action and commitment be established based on the principles that shared perspectives bring about common meaning, and potentiate collaborative and participatory action.

Finally, there is a striking similarity between the palaver process, *ịkpá ńkàtá* – exploring the vast array of wisdom of the ancestors through creating an expansive space for dialogue in the community – and *ịkpá ǹkàtà* (the art of basket making). These are similar words, whose distinction can only be made through the tonal inflection of native Igbo speakers. It can also be metaphorized as plotting against someone, in many instances, as a way of fighting back to undermine those who maintain unjust structures in the community or in inter-personal relationship.

However, beyond this metaphorized meaning, this phrase shows the heart of the palaver in Igboland as the art of weaving vast streams of perspectives, and crafting wisdom and insights into a new event of meaning. "Basket making is done by intertwining of the fibrous materials derived from the palm branches. The fibrous tread is got from the palm branches and kept for two or three days so as to enhance its elasticity. The fibre from the dorsal surface which is thick, is used for farming while the light ventral surface is used on the intertwining process – "*ịkpà – arịa* or "*ǹkàtà.*"'"[10] In the same way, the palaver in Igboland, like basket-making requires an intertwining art of conversation which is open to diversity of perspectives; is tolerant of differences – *uche onye adighi ya njo; uche bu akpa, onye o bula nya nke ya*; *onye kwuo uche ya* (opinions are like handbag of many treasurers that everyone is carrying with him or her). This weaving together of perspectives helps the community to interpret history and advance the possibility for the emergence of a consensus and resolution in inter-personal relationships and other forms of relationships. Indeed, at the end of a successful palaver, people say: *yábụ ǹkàtà ànyị kpàrà ághọọlá ńgịgá* – (we have closed the deal or literally, we have weaved the wicker basket into a hamper).[11] Indeed, the palaver among the Igbo is figuratively referred to as *ibọri ụka,* which has the same roots as sharing (*ibọ anụ*) in a game, the art of dividing or sharing a meat. Truth is our collective prize, and commitment to the truth and to realizing or implementing the final decision is like sharing in a meal.

The food analogy points to one way out of many through which the African palaver can be inculturated in both the African churches who are also struggling with finding the right path for dialogue and discerning differences in a healthy way and in the Catholic Church caught in new forms of Manichean dualism that has created seemingly unbridgeable camps between progressives and traditionalists. Like traditional African society, Christian communities can come together around the table of the Eucharist and in multiple sites of hope and pain in the world today. The community comes together to eat of the Word that gives life; everyone should be welcomed to this sacred space. People come not with pre-packaged notions of truth, absolute statements, and certainties, but with an openness to listen to each other's stories and the humility which can bring about conversion of perspectives and healing of distortions in one's thinking and acting as a result of human limitations. The coming together is an invitation to participate in listening, discerning, engaging in the search for solutions through an openness to the surprises of the Holy Spirit. Decisions made at the end are definitive but not framed in absolute terms thus leaving room for further deliberation and consideration.

However, because decisions are made in a participative way, everyone sees themselves in the decision made and takes ownership in the collective effort in walking and working together in implementing them.

Notes

1. Chinua Achebe, *Things Fall Apart*. NY: Anchor Books, 1994, 7.
2. Achebe, 7-8.
3. Masamba ma Mpolo, "Jesus Christ—Word of Life: An African Contribution to the Theme of the Sixth Assembly" *The Ecumenical Review*, 35, no. 2 (April, 1983), 168.
4. *Ibid.*, 168-169.
5. *Ibid.,* 169.
6. Gerald Adewole, "The Art of Conversation: Proverbs in the Achebe's *Things Fall Apart*", *The Republic*, Vol. 4, No. 1 (December,2019-January, 2020), 6.
7. *Ibid.*, 28.
8. Achebe, 141.
9. Pope Francis, Ceremony Commemorating the 50th Anniversary of the Institution of the Synod of Bishops, AAS, 107 (2015), 1141.
10. Sabastine Chidozie Agu and George Okagu, "An Ethno-Archaeologiccal Perspective on Oil Palm Tree (Elaeis guineensis Jacq) in Old Nsukka Division of Enugu State", *IKENGA International Journal of African Studies*, Vol. 15, April, 2013, 8.
11. I wish to acknowledge the input of Dr Ohajuobodo Oko, and Fr Ikenna Ekekwe for the translation and transcription of the Igbo words used here.

Formal Synodality in Action: Beyond the Gulf Between Consultative and Deliberative

ALPHONSE BORRAS

The 'purely' consultative nature of many ecclesial bodies has become problematic in the eyes of many Catholics. The democratic ethos and their ecclesial awareness lead to them making a legitimate request to be heard in questions which concern the Church and the proclamation of the Gospel. How should decision-making processes, which honour the shared responsibility of all the baptised, as well as the freedom of the minister who is the guarantor of ecclesial communion, be achieved ? The ecclesiological scope of synodality in action sheds light on the limitations of the 'consultatif-deliberative' word pair. It enables us to broaden the field of what is canonically possible while honouring the pneumatological dimension of the ecclesial community through the distinction between decision-making and decision-taking.

The term 'synodality' is an abstract concept. This issue deals with 'synodalities'. The plural suggests a range of practicalities, but also a diversity of doctrinal approaches among canon lawyers just as much as among theologians.[1] My article will focus on formal synodality, in other words, on the formalised ways of its implementation which reflects institutional loci as much as procedures or 'participatory processes', whose objective, as Pope Francis reminds us in passing, is not 'ecclesiastical organisation but the missionary aspiration of reaching everyone' (*Evangelii Gaudium* [henceforth *EG*] 31). This formalisation of synodality presupposes an informal synodality which flows from the baptised 'journeying together'. On hearing the Word of God, the baptised discern the work of the Spirit of God in the signs of the times and in the heart of history to bring this world to its completion.[2]

In this light, in virtue of their baptism and according to their individual charisms, all Christ's faithful are jointly responsible, each according to their role, to proclaim, celebrate, and be a witness to the Gospel as the Good News of God's love for every human being, without exception or exclusion. This shared responsibility indicates the baptised as individuals, whereas the concept of synodality indicates a constitutive aspect of the Church as a community. What is more, there is a plurality of synodalities, just as there are differences between the shared responsibilities of the baptised due to the diversity of their charisms.

The 'purely' consultative nature of several ecclesial bodies has become problematic in the eyes of many Catholics, who feel that they are not being heard by their pastors, particularly where, in addition, they have previously been disappointed by sterile exchanges and discussions without results. Canon law can shed light on this by enabling us to grasp the ecclesiological meaning of synodality *in action* and the decision-making processes as well as the limitations of the pair 'consultative-deliberative', which it is important to consider when honouring the pneumatological aspect of the ecclesial community.

I What is my approach?

My article pertains to the teachings of canon law and deals with ecclesiastical institutions from the perspective of the regulations on social *behaviours*, in other words, the relationships between the faithful and institutions. Church law is a juridical provision for the proper character of community life in the Church, its *Zusammenleben* as much as its *Gemeinwesen*. It deals with juridical actions – those actions which have consequences in the field of law, for individuals as much as for institutions, from the perspective of the protection and promotion of ecclesiastical communion.[3] It is restricted to protecting the membership of believers, the proclamation of the Gospel which it presupposes, and the ecclesiastical incorporation which it implies.

These clarifications are important because in the contemporary language of many Catholics their spontaneous approach to the Church and its institutions often functions through the sociology of organisations, social anthropology, or even civil law. On the point under discussion here, cultural presuppositions and, in particular, the democratic ethos of our societies determine how Catholics look at their life in the Church and the range of its communities. At this level there is a gap between the requirements of modernity and the practices of *the Church* in terms of the participation of the faithful in ecclesial life and in the testimony of the Gospel.

In this matter, the law of the Catholic Church must broaden the field of what is canonically possibly. Theologically, from the perspective of faith, the Church is the people whom God has won over and whom he gathers together and sends out as the ecclesial body of Christ and the temple of the Holy Spirit. In its very origins the Church is communion, that is, participation (Latin, *cum-munus*) in the life of grace by the breaking into history of a God who offers humanity his covenant, sealed definitively in the incarnation, passion, and resurrection of the Word and the coming of the Spirit at Pentecost.

This communion is organic in terms of the diversity of its members in the variety of charisms, states of life, vocations, capacities, service and ministries, and so forth (cf. *LG* 7c; 12b; 32a.c; cc. 204 § 1, 208, 211; etc.). To describe it as 'synodal' is to no longer emphasise its organic character but rather its dynamic dimension, for all the baptized are called to play their part in communicating the Gospel.

II Synodality: a Church which convenes

Synodality is not purely a mimesis of the democratic ethos, but this makes the ecclesial community even more sensitive to the participation in its mission of all the faithful, together and individually according to their charisms and roles. Synodality therefore can and must be deployed from a participatory ecclesiology: informally when everyone is on the same journey countering the temptation to 'walk alone' (*EG* 33); formally through institutional mediation at every level and in every aspect of ecclesial life but first and foremost starting from and within the local diocesan Church (*SC* 41a; *LG* 23a and 26a; *CD* 11; *AG* 15; cc. 368 and 369), and by extension the whole local and localised community, whether hierarchical or associative, including religious communities.[4]

In the organic communion of the Church with its various and complementary charisms, those ministers ordained to preside in the Church and at its Eucharist – bishops and priests – are by virtue of this constituted for the service of the people of God (cf. c. 1008) in virtue of the authority 'by which Christ builds up, sanctifies, and rules his Body' (*PO* 2c; cf. *LG* 21 and 28). At the same time they prove that they encourage the Church's fundamental apostolicity, that is, its rooting in the apostolic faith and fidelity to the Gospel. According to the words of the Council Fathers, 'they also know that they were not ordained by Christ to take upon themselves alone the entire salvific mission of the Church toward the world.' (*LG* 30) Pastors do not do everything in the Church because they have neither all the charisms nor all the gifts of the Spirit to proclaim the Gospel.

In a more pneumatological key, the Council Fathers continued their words in positive terms: 'they understand that it is their noble duty to shepherd the faithful and to recognize their ministries and charisms so that all according to their proper roles may cooperate in this common undertaking with one mind' (Latin, *ut cuncti suo modo ad commune opus unanimiter cooperentur*, *LG* 30). The people of God have been entrusted to them, but are not their property. The Spirit distributes his gifts widely among the people at the same time as he inspires the faithful in their triple priestly, prophetic, and kingly offices, in other words, in exercising the mission which God has entrusted to the Church that it may carry out this mission in the world (cf. *LG* 31a; c. 204 § 1).

By virtue of their baptism and even more of their ordination, the pastors are 'under the Word of God' (the rite of placing the book of the Gospels on the head of the bishop at his consecration!) and know how to listen to it to discern, with the other faithful, what the Spirit is saying to the Churches (cf. Acts 2.7, 11, 17, 29; 3.6,13, 22) and the path which the Saviour is pointing out to them to follow together (cf. *EG* 20). But since they alone are not the whole Church, but rather are part of the body along with the faithful entrusted to them, pastors must first listen to the faithful, with a view to taking their counsel, not paternalistically but while respecting what they are.

III Listen, seek an opinion, obtain consent

With regard to pastors, listening is an obligation of the role, and not merely an obligation of charity,[5] which they exercise without ever forgetting that they share their status as baptized people with all. Of course, this listening takes place day to day in the interpersonal relationships between the pastor and the faithful whom he encounters as individuals, but also with them as a group, collectively. This collective listening is the most appropriate for the faithful and their pastors together, as the ecclesial body within which all take their part in a differentiated way, under the influence of the Spirit which is given to everyone.

This requires a mutual listening exchange between everyone in the image of the practice of 'endless discussions' which are found in virtually every culture, at every level of the social, commercial, economic, or political life of individuals involved in some kind of collective enterprise. These discussions very often involve negotiations or transactions which in themselves show that everyone is concerned to some degree or other, in principle. Is this spontaneously the case in the day to day life of ecclesial communities?

From the perspective of canon law, it is important that this synodality be formalised 'in action'. There is the basic level of mutual listening between all the faithful, including pastors and superiors, and there is the higher level where the pastor (or superior) not only listens, but seeks advice from the community or the faithful. In this way he shows more clearly that he truly considers them to be members of the ecclesial body on the basis of the differentiated participation of everyone. What is more, by asking for advice, the pastor can no longer act as though he has not heard them. He is in some way more 'obliged' to listen, that is, more connected to what he 'wanted' to hear. Asking for an opinion commits the person who does the asking, as we shall see below.

In addition to these two stages of being prepared to listen and asking for an opinion, there is a third, which is to obtain consent. At this level, the pastor (or superior) is truly obliged by the consent of all, whether collectively (cf c.127§ 1) or individually (cf. c. 127 § 2, 1°). These are the three stages of a growing formalisation of synodality in which 'all according to their proper roles may cooperate in this undertaking with one mind' (*LG* 30).

This *opus commune* relates to the proclamation of the Gospel, the (in) coming Kingdom of God of which the Church is the sign and the seed. It is to this end that the ecclesial community meets. This happens formally through both consultation and deliberation, which both lead to decisions being taken. From the perspective of the institution which implements one or the other of these methods, in canon law we would speak about consultative or deliberative bodies. These rely on the consent or approval of all, with all opinions carrying equal weight.[6]

In the universal law of the 1983 Code for Catholics of the Latin rite, in addition to canon 127 which deals with the consensus needed by a superior to place an act, there is the question of the consent of the college of consultors (cc. 272, 485, 500 § 2, 1018 § 1,2°, 1277, 1292 §§ 1-4), of the agreement of those who legitimately claim rights, principally in terms of historic property (cc. 174, 1222 § 2, 1277, 1292 §§ 1-4, 1524 § 2), and of the consent of the Council of the superior or moderator in consecrated life (cc. 638 § 3, 647, 665 § 1, 684 § 1, 686 §§ 1 and 3, 688 § 2, 690, 703, 726 § 2, 743, 744 § 1, 745, 1018 § 1,2°). In institutes of consecrated life (cc. 573-720) and societies of apostolic life (cc. 731-755), as well as private or public associations of the faithful (cc. 298-329), the assent of the members is generally required for major questions about the life and governance of these institutions in conformity with their proper statutes and constitutions.

In addition to these canons, in terms of local diocesan Churches, with the exception of election to an office or a title (cf. cc. 164-179), there is no mention of the need for individual or collective consent to solve a problem or take a decision. Generally speaking, deliberative suffrage is in reality the prerogative of bishops at the level of groups of local Churches or of the universal Church,[7] except as we have seen in institutes of consecrated life, societies of apostolic life, and associations of the faithful.

In other words, in the 1983 Code, we have to note that generally there is a regrettable minimalism for the involvement of the baptized in the deliberative model, at least in diocesan and especially in parish life,[8] where their role is not exercised at all in deliberative bodies.

IV The ecclesiological limitations of 'purely consultative'

On the other hand the faithful may – at least in principle – exercise, by means of consultation, their duty of counsel towards pastors (cf. cc. 275 § 2 and 529 § 2) or collectively meet with them to clarify questions, resolve problems, or undertake particular actions (cf. c. 228 § 2), if their pastors ask them to. In this case, this takes place within the councils established for these purposes where through dialogue a common will is forged among all the faithful including the pastors. The Code allows for these bodies by clarifying that the faithful only have a consultative voice (Lat. *votum tantum consultivum*): this is the case for a diocesan Synod (c. 466) or in the diocesan (c. 514 § 1) or parish (c. 536 § 1) pastoral Councils; priests, too, only have a consultative voice within the council of priests (c. 500 § 2).

This restrictive expression (Lat. *tantum*) raises problems for many faithful who see it as a disqualification of their differentiated participation in the *opus commune* to the advantage of a great number of pastors within the ecclesial body, while the Spirit distributes his gifts to everyone according to ability, throughout the Church. Theologically speaking this restrictive expression does not honour the *sensus fidei fidelium*, that 'smell of the sheep' to 'find new ways' (cf. *EG* 31; cf. *LG* 12a *in credendo falli nequit*). The teaching of canon law promotes the protection of the freedom of the pastor, whether bishop or priest, by virtue of his ordination to preside in the church and at the Eucharist. This places him in 'opposition' to the other faithful at the same time as being a guarantee of the apostolicity of their faith in communion with the whole Church. Pastors are in a position of otherness within the ecclesial community, not of outsiders! The expression *tantum consultivum* appears even more inappropriate from the ecclesiological perspective as it places pastors in a position of superiority – verticality – and reinforces the ecclesial marginalisation of the faithful.

How can we strengthen the role of the faithful? Just as the community is not 'not without' its pastor, so the pastor is not 'not without' the community. The symbolic link is more forcefully expressed here through the double negation. Are they not all stakeholders in the decision-making process?

Fortunately canon law itself corrects the minimalist import of *tantum consultivum*, for when a superior requires the counsel of a group (Lat. *coetus*) or of a college (Lat. *collegium*), he must seek the counsel of all members for his consultation to be valid. This is prescribed in canon 127 § 1. In other words, the superior can not proceed in an eclectic or selective manner, but must seek advice from the group or the college as such, or his consultation is invalid, it is null and void. Here we can truly see how to seeking counsel goes beyond simply listening! This also applies in a consultation of persons as individuals: by virtue of canon 127 § 2, it is invalid if the superior does not seek their opinion. However this same canon also prescribes that 'although in no way obliged to accede to their recommendation, even if unanimous, nevertheless the superior should not act contrary to it, especially when there is a consensus' (c. 127 § 2,2° ; cf. CIC 1917 c. 105). This measure may be applied in the case of collective consultation (c. 127 § 1) by virtue of the principal of canonical equity (cf. c. 19).

V Decision-making and decision-taking

The norm established by canon 127 § 2 2° is of capital importance for this article! I would formulate as follows: the superior must follow the consensus of advice of the people he consults, unless he has an overwhelming reason not to do so. Even though he is not juridically forced to do so, in general he should follow advice as consensus. Two Roman documents agree with this direction.

The 1997 Instruction *In Constitutione apostolica* on diocesan synods explains the 'consultative' nature 'to indicate that the bishop remains free to accept or not the recommendations made to him', while also recalling that the synod members are not 'external', for 'they collaborate actively in drawing up [its] declarations and decrees'.[9] Let us focus here on the verb 'drawing up'. Further on, the instructions says that 'the Bishop *always remains free* to determine what weight is to be attributed to their results. Consequently, he may wish to accept the common view shared by the members of the Synod, unless there should exist some grave obstacle to be evaluated by him *coram Domino*' (IV.5b).

The 2004 directory on the pastoral duties of bishops[10] emphasises 'the organic nature of ecclesial communion and ... the structure of participation' (165) and, in the sense of canon 127 § 2 2°, prescribes that the bishop is not 'to dissociate himself from opinions and votes expressed by a large majority, except for grave doctrinal, disciplinary, or liturgical reasons.'

(171a).

In a consultative body, the faithful who are approached by their pastors to do so give their opinion in order to draw up together with their pastors decisions about the life, governance, witness, and mission of the community. The social sciences offer us a very useful distinction here to honour the pneuatological dimension of the shared baptismal responsibility of each person, each according to their charisms, without prejudice to the ministerial presiding role of pastors. This is the distinction between 'decision-making' and 'decision-taking'.

This process of collective decision-making is in the scope of/part of time and relies on several factors, both objective and subjective: the final decision taken is of course the aim of the process where there is no need to reach a majority agreement first, but rather to verify the degree of agreement among those concerned. This is also a gauge of the reception of the decision, matured by a discernment of God's will in reaching the agreement of all. While not stipulated in the Code, the particular law of a local Church must allow for the fact that in its pastoral Councils, the community concerned and their pastor will reach a decision he, the pastor, must take. Stipulating this in canon law would be an initial defence against a drift towards individualism and authoritarianism.

By virtue of its fundamental synodality and as a subject of action and by right, the ecclesial community participates in the decision-making which is to be taken by the pastoral authority. As guarantors of the apostolicity of lived and professed faith, pastors sanction this decision through the seal of communion with other communities and with the Church as a whole. In so doing, they do not create the community's apostolicity, but authenticate its fidelity to the Gospel, and in this way they recognise the legitimate role of the faithful, who can say, *res nostra agitur*.

Translated by Patricia and Liam Kelly

Notes

1. Among canon lawyers there are already nuances leading to a diversity of approaches. For instance, compare Michel Dortel-Claudot, 'L'évêque et la synodalité dans le nouveau

Code de droit canonique', *Nouvelle Revue Théologique* 106 (1984), 641-657; Eugenio Corecco, 'Sinodalità', in Giuseppe Barbaglio & Severino Dianich (eds.), *Nuovo Dizionario di Teologia,* 6th ed., Cinisello Balsamo. Ed. Paoline, 1991, 1431-1456; Norbert Witsch, 'Synodalität', in Axel von Campenhausen, Ilona Riedel-Spangenberger & Reinhold Sebott (eds.), *Lexikon für Kirchen- und Staatskirchenrecht* t. 3, Paderborn-München-Wien-Zürich, F. Schöningh, 2000, 642-644; Manoelo Agusto Santos, 'Sinodalidad', in Javier Otaduy, Antonio Viana & Joaquín Sedano (eds.), *Diccionario general de derecho canónico*, vol. 7, Pamplona, Universidad de Navarra – Thomson Reuters Aranzadi, 2012, 341-345.

2. In this article I shall refer mainly to Alphonse Borras, 'La synodalité du Peuple de Dieu', *Prêtres diocésains* n° 1337-1138 (March-April 1996), 263-280; '*Votum tantum consultivum*: les limites ecclésiologiques d'une formule canonique', *Didaskalia* 45 (2015/1), 145-162; *Communion ecclésiale et synodalité*, with a preface by Charles Theobald, Paris, Éd. CLD, 'Cahiers de la NRT', 2018; 'La synodalité ecclésiale: diversité de lieux et interactions mutuelles', *Recherches de Science religieuse* 107/2 (2019), 275-299.

3. Cf. Jean-Marc Bahans, *La nature du droit canonique. Essai de théorie et de théologie du droit*, Les Presses Universitaires – Institut catholique de Toulouse, 2019.

4. I am thinking first of all of the local diocesan Church (diocesan synod, pastoral council, council of priests, etc), and everything which goes to make that up, primarily the parish communities (pastoral council), as well as the range of associations, including associations of consecrated life (with their internal bodies for participation and governance). Then there are the groupings of local Churches, such as an ecclesial province (particular and provincial councils) or within a nation (Bishops' conference), and the level of the continent (CELAM, CCEE and similar bodies in Africa, Asia, and Oceania) as well as that of the Church as a whole (principally the Synod of bishops).

5. By all accounts, we note in passing that listening is required of all the faithful, every single one, reflecting the concern we all have for one another; in these terms it is an *obligation of charity*.

6. In this sense, the adjective 'deliberative' describes the vote of individuals (as physical persons) within the body concerned (a moral person described in canon law as a juridical person). This is said to be 'deliberative' and all its members decide, with equal votes, on the basis of a relative or an absolute majority, or a simple or qualified majority.

7. L'absence de protagonisme des fidèles laïcs est encore plus flagrante sur le plan d'un regroupement d'Églises particulières. Les évêques ont un suffrage délibératif dans les conciles particuliers et Conférences épiscopales, mais les décisions qu'ils approuvent doivent reposer sur une majorité qualifiée, et sont soumises à des modalités de *recognitio* par le Siège apostolique (cc. 445 et 455 § 2). Et enfin, sur le plan de l'Église universelle, les évêques en concile œcuménique ont voix délibérative mais les décrets conciliaires doivent être approuvés par le pape en union avec les pères conciliaires, confirmés et approuvés par lui (cf. c. 341 § 1) ; en dehors d'un concile les décrets du collège des évêques ont besoin de cette confirmation et promulgation pontificale (cf. c. 341 § 2). Quant au Synode des évêques, il n'a pouvoir délibératif que sur concession du pape (cf. c. 343).

8. Cf. Ugo Sartorio, 'Sinodalità per una Chiesa in riforma', *Studia Patavina* 66 (2019), 279-292.

9. Congregation for Bishops and Congregation for the evangelisation of peoples, 'Instruction on diocesan synods', (1997), 2.

10. Congregation for Bishops, *Directory* Apostolorum successores *for the pastoral ministry of bishops*, 2004.

Part Three: Founding and Sustaining a Synodal Church

Synodality as a Constitutive Dimension of the Church and an Expression of the Gospel

GILLES ROUTHIER

The boy who cried wolf found that one day, when he was really in danger, no one took his cries seriously. In the same way, thanks to calling in season and out of season on synodality, and making it into a trendy slogan, we no longer realise that it is connatural with the Church itself, being an essential characteristic of that Church. Far from being a trend, synodality is a requirement, because given what it is, the Church is called to materialise in the synodal principle and to live synodally. For the Church this is not about conforming to the signs of the times, but rather, in an ongoing conversion, to become that which it truly is.

As Jean-Marie Tillard observed, the life of the Church is subject to trends, so many sprees of concern which never succeed in long-term conversion. At the end of the 1960s it was all about 'co-responsibility', the idea emphasised by Cardinal Suenens. Then the 1980s imposed a new theme, that of 'communion', before, at the start of 2000s, attention suddenly turned towards the hermeneutics of Vatican II. Today there is a great risk of making synodality the new magic word which will be here today and gone tomorrow.

This is a real risk, and, since what goes up must come down, the thoughtless and improper use of the term synodality could lead to it being reduced to a slogan, emptying it of its meaning. I therefore plead for a rigorous, moderate use of the term, as I consider the development of a synodal model of Church governance too important. The stakes are high and we cannot reduce synodality to a passing fashion. Here I shall try to demonstrate that synodality represents a constitutive dimension of the Church and an expression of the Gospel.

I Synodality as a constitutive dimension of the Church

Catholic theology's re-appropriation of the term synodality is relatively recent,[1] dating really from the post-conciliar period. This is not surprising since it was the synodal experience in itself which enabled a new awareness of the conciliar or synodal nature of the Church. As H.J. Pottemeyer wrote about the development of communion ecclesiology, 'a practice and experience of communion are necessary for a corresponding ecclesiology to be able to develop and to be accepted. The formation of communion ecclesiology within the council itself is a prime example of the intimate union between the practice and experience of communion, on the one hand, and theoretical reflection on this and its formulation, on the other.'[2] The link between the fact of the synod and the awareness of the Church's basic synodality is not a Catholic phenomenon. As M. Stavrou has demonstrated, in tracing the emergence of synodality in the ecclesial awareness of the Christian East, the Eastern Churches lived out a synodal ethos well before the consequent ecclesiology was thematized. For him, it was only relatively late, in the mid-nineteenth century, that the Slavophile movement undertook an ecclesiological reflection on conciliarity and the doctrine of *sobornost,* which would influence Catholic ecclesiologists and ecumenists, particularly Y. Congar.

Theology's late appropriation of the term synodality, and its even later acceptance by the magisterium of the Catholic Church might lead us to think that it is a novelty. What is more, we might believe that its appearance is linked to the democratic ethos of western societies, and that synodality therefore does not belong to the nature of the Church, or is not a constitutive dimension of it. Those who seek to establish synodality as a constitutional principle of the Church by emphasising the constant practice of its synodal activity are opposed by those who say that councils and synods only appear in the third century and that, consequently, Church governance and the exercise of authority in the Church are not linked to the synodal principle, or that the synodal way of government is but one possibility among others.

However a decisive study carried out by the World Council of Churches led to a more nuanced conclusion. According to this study, conciliarity/ synodality 'is a constant structure of the Church, a dimension which belongs to its nature'[3] and, for the period which precedes that of the formal calling of synodal meetings, one can certainly, with Jean Zizioulas, speak about the 'primitive conciliarity', linked to the liturgical life of an *Ecclesia*, the *synodos* emerging gradually from the *synaxis* until it became its extension.[4]

Going beyond the binary thought patterns which force us to make an exclusive choice between two terms, the first Faith and Order world conference held in Lausanne in 1927 would establish a balance between three constitutional principles: the personal, the collegial, and the synodal.

We find the role of the bishop in the constitution of the early Church along with the Councils of Elders and the Community of the Faithful. Each of these three systems of ecclesial organisation (episcopalian, presbyterian, and congregationalist) has been accepted in the past over centuries, and is still practised today by major groups within Christianity. Consequently we feel that, under certain conditions which remain to be clarified, they should all take their respective places in the organisation of the reunited Church.[5]

Thus, while not exclusive, the synodal principle was part of the Church's make up from the very beginning. This vision would later be repeated in the majority of great texts produced by bilateral and multilateral ecumenical commissions.[6]

In turn several theologians would maintain that the 'synodal essence' belongs to the nature of the Church. This was especially true of Yves Congar who emphasised that 'the conciliar principle is essentially linked to the nature of the Church.'[7] Several others would reach similar conclusions, particularly H.-M. Legrand who talks about the 'Church's synodal dimension' and the 'Church's essential conciliarity',[8] while P. Neuner emphasises that 'it is only this (synodal) form which corresponds to the Church's self-understanding as maintained once again by the Second Vatican Council, and as it is founded in the New Testament writings and in the original tradition of the Church.'[9] While reserving judgement on the concept of synodality,[10] J. Ratzinger does recognise 'the Church's collegial structure', describing a similar reality, the interdependence linking a bishop to his presbyterium and his community,[11] a relationship which gives structure to the Church.

Several canon lawyers share this opinion.[12] According to them, conciliarity and synodality belong to the very nature of the Church although, these principles have been expressed in various ways through history. Here we again have Congar's useful distinction between the conciliar and synodal structure of the Church, and its concrete government, where institutional figures and synodal practices express the synodal nature of the Church in a particular time and culture. Thus while the council is only a specific service in the Church, as demonstrated by Ratzinger, and is only called occasionally, this does not negate the synodal nature of the Church which finds expression in other institutional forms.

The Church's synodal nature is also recognised by several theologians in other Christian traditions. In Waldensian theology for instance, we note the statement of P. Rica that 'all organised expressions of Christianity realise a certain form of conciliarity: Christianity in nearly all its versions appears to be constitutionally conciliar.'[13] From the Orthodox, we see, among others, A. Scrima, who observes that, 'In the East, "conciliarity" is present with the Church: it arises, as it were, with its mysterious foundations. We may almost say we have a tautology: the Church is conciliar because it is the Church, because it is a living communion in Christ.'[14] G. Larentzakis shares this opinion, stating that 'the Church without synodality is a contradiction in terms, as etymology shows that the terms "Ekklesia", "synod", and "council" have almost the same meaning.'[15] W. Aymans, on the contrary, claims 'that the synods of the Orthodox Church have a constitutive significance for the constitution of the Church, while in constitutional Latin law they have more of an organisational nature.'[16]

II Synodality as an expression of the Gospel

Here we should not understand the Gospel as a writing in which we can locate the reality of synodality, since we cannot find the term itself there. The Gospel is the Good News of the Kingdom which erupts into the world in the person of Jesus. What we can observe there for certain is the conversion of the idea of the practice of authority which arrives in the person of Jesus. The master makes himself a servant and a slave, washing the feet of his disciples (Jn 13.13). He asks them not to call him Rabbi, reminding them that they are all brothers (Mt 23. 8-10), teaching them that the disciple is not greater than the master (Lk 6.40), cutting short discussions about who was the greater among them (Mk 9.34) and rejecting the request of the mother of the sons of Zebedee for the best places for her sons (Mt 20.21), and looking with amusement at those guests who rush to take the best places at a banquet (Lk. 14.7ff). In short, it is the raising up of the humble and loss of power by the powerful proclaimed in the Magnificat which happens in complete freedom.

The usual outlines and representations of power and authority are smashed to pieces. These ways of thinking and acting no longer hold. They are out of date. The out-dating of the familiar and ways and the received ways of thinking about power and of exercising it are at the heart of the Gospel which works social connections and the kinds of relations in among people. The disciples are called to continue and reproduce what arrived with the person of Jesus; thus, 'If I the Lord and Master have washed your feet, you too must wash each other's feet'. (Jn 13.14) Through living in his company they learned that 'whoever wants to be great among you will be your servant', and 'whoever wants to be the first among you will be the slave of all'. (Mk 10.42-44)

They mastered this new way of acting and this converted conception of authority so well that in the *Ekklesia* they developed the habit of using the term 'brother' to describe one another.[17] Synodality, which builds up an interdependence between the person exercising the ministry of presiding and all the members of the Church, added to the exercise of authority the duty to listen, dialogue, search for opinions, consult, and bear witness on the plan of action, this evangelical conversion of authority. This cannot be exercised in a solitary and autocratic manner. The word of one person must include the voice of the whole Church; no one in the Church is *totus* by themselves.

The book of the Acts of the Apostles suggests a particular kind of relationships between the members of the Church which are characteristic of synodality: the structured and organic cooperation of everyone, presided over by the apostles, with an eye to joint action. No one acts alone, but everyone must rather act in solidarity. Every time there is a crisis or an important decision to be taken, the Church is called together, the Spirit invoked, there is discussion, discernment, and the decision which is reached is taken. This was already happening in Acts 6, where we can see the resolution of the first crisis – a crisis of growth – in the Church. The massive increase in the number of disciples, the appearance of different groups (Hellenists and Jews), and the inability of the earliest organisation to offer material assistance and charity – the support of widows – provoked a real crisis which almost split the community into two, with the Hellenists tempted to create their own group with its own organisation. In other words, we can see that the dissent between groups of diverging tendencies and the murmuring and recrimination of the Hellenists bear witness to tensions in the Church. So, 'the Twelve called the disciples together' (Acts 6.2) The disciples asked the whole church to seek out seven brothers to give them an office (v. 3) and it was the members of the Church who chose Stephen, Philip, and the others, (v. 5) presenting them to the apostles to lay hands on them. (v. 6) In Acts 15, which introduces the so-called Council of Jerusalem, we see the same kind of relationship when, in a game of interdependence, each actor plays his role, while listening to the others. Here again the Church is called together and it is in this coming together in which the question under debate is resolved. In this way everyone becomes present at both events, no one goes it alone, no one decides alone. Thus the synodal principle, without obliterating the personal and collegial principles, is shown as the constitutional principle of the Church which is at heart an assembly in which the participation of every member must be honoured. In the emerging Church as presented in the book of Acts, there is a basic practice which is to call the Church together to report or expose the facts of the problem, to permit the assembly to express itself, and to submit the decision, which emerges from this process of exchange, listening, and discernment, to the assembly. In summary, in the context of the Empire of the first centuries, the *Ekklesia* found an original way of governance which assumed the conversion of the idea of authority and the exercise of power which the proclamation of the Gospel of the Kingdom involved.

III Conclusion

The concept of synodality describes a typical form of relationships between persons, one characterised by interdependence, in the field ecclesial governance. This principle involves the coming together as an assembly, the participation of all in an organised deliberative process, cooperation in exchange, mutual dialogue and listening, and collaboration in communion, presided over by the bishop. Synodality presupposes an effort, for everyone must pull their weight, demonstrate solidarity, and have desire to end up with consensus, a shared conviction. It presupposes the desire to collaborate, to accept and agree, to give and receive. In its strongest sense it describes a right which calls for procedures, deliberative practices, and institutional forms. It also calls to attitudes. Down the centuries, according to cultural contexts and places, this basic synodality has been expressed in a range of ways. It has been expressed through a concrete system of councils and assemblies (local and general synods), and borrowed procedures and deliberative processes from cultures. Synodality, the constitutive dimension of the Church, is joined in an ever-delicate balance with the personal and collegial principles, the three forming a tripod and the three principles being correlative. The history of the Christian Churches teaches us that any reduction in one principle always corresponds to an imbalance. Synodality is not a structure in the Church which functions as a counterweight to an initial personal structure. In the synodal exercise of government, the two constitutive elements, the ministry and the participation of all, are inseparable. We must therefore neither establish an opposition between them, nor let them function in parallel, but join them together.

Translated Patricia and Liam Kelly

Notes

1. At the start of the 1990s I carried out an extensive literature review on this question, and found very few works on synodality before 1970. See Gilles Routhier, 'La synodalité de l'Église locale', *Studia canonica*, 26 (1992), p. 111-161.
2. Hermann J. Pottmeyer, 'Continuité et innovation dans l'ecclésiologie de Vatican II. L'influence de Vatican I sur l'ecclésiologie de Vatican II et la nouvelle réception de Vatican I à la lumière de Vatican II, in Giuseppe Alberigo (ed.), *Les Églises après Vatican II,* Paris, Beauchesne (Théologie historique 61), 1981, p. 93.
3. Faith and Order, 'The Importance of the Conciliar Process in the Ancient Church for the Ecumenical Movement', *Councils and the Ecumenical Movement,* WC Studies 5,

Geneva, 1968, p. 10.

4. John D. Zizioulas, 'The Development of Conciliar Structures to the Time of First Ecumenical Movement', in *Councils and the Ecumenical Movement,* p. 34-51. On the birth of synods, see too E. Lanne according to whom, 'if in the life of the Church at the turn of the 2nd and 3rd centuries the meeting of synods represents something externally new, it remains the case that in its intention it is no different from other instruments of communion between the Churches since the very beginning : exchange of letters, hospitality given to brothers from other Churches, sharing in the same Eucharist, the reception of the same canonical Scriptures.' (Jacques-Emmanuel Lanne, 'L'origine des synodes', *Theologische Zeischrift* 27 (1971), p. 219.) Thus at a particular point the formal synod became the means of expression of that need belonging to the nature of the Church, of building, protecting, and expressing the communion which constitutes its very being.

5. On Baptism, Eucharist, and Ministry ('BEM'), see Faith and Order, *Proceedings of the World Conference Lausanne,* New York, Doubleday, 1928, p. 469.

6. The final report of the Anglican-Roman Catholic International Commission notes a convergence on principles of primacy, conciliarity, and synodality. See 'Authority in the Church I: Venice, 1976', 9, 19-23; 'Elucidation of "Authority in the Church I"', 5; 'Authority in the Church II: Windsor, 1981', 28, 33. Even more systematically, the members of the Lutheran-Roman Catholic Commission on Unity created a link between personal responsibility, the synodality of the local Church, and the conciliarity of the Churches ('Facing Unity', 1985, 112-114). See this again in the Faith and Order 1982 BEM document, n° 26.

7. 'Remarques sur le concile comme assemblée et sur la conciliarité foncière de l'Église', in *Le concile au jour le jour, deuxième session*, Paris, Cerf, 1964, p. 39. See too 'Conclusion', in *Le Concile et les conciles. Contribution à l'histoire de la vie conciliaire de l'Église*, Paris, Cerf, 1960, p. 308-310. In this latter text Congar uses the term conciliarity rather than synodality, as was the case in the ecumenical movement at the time, as well as the Slavophile movement, both of which he was in close contact with. See too his later article in the same direction, 'Structure ou régime conciliaire de l'Église', *Concilium* 187 (1983), p. 15-20.

8. Hervé-M. Legrand, 'Synodes et conseils de l'après-concile. Quelques enjeux ecclésiologiques', *Nouvelle Revue Théologique* 98/3 (1976), p. 193. Elsewhere he wrote that synodality 'is part of the fundamental nature of the Church' ('Grâce et institution dans l'Église. Les fondements théologiques du droit canonique', in *L'Église institution et foi,* Bruxelles, Presses de l'Université Saint-Louis, 1984, p. 164.

9. Peter Neuner, *Synodales Prinzip. Der grössere Spielraum im Kirchenrecht*, Herder, Freiburg, 1973, p. 92; see too p. 9.

10. The reservations turn on the concept of *synedrion* and was expressed in the context of an old polemical exchange (1961) with H. Küng, who established a relationship of shared interiority between '*the Church* as ecumenical council called together by God', and 'the *ecumenical council* called together by men as a representation of the ecumenical council called together by God' (*ThQ* 141 [1961], pp. 56, 60). J. Ratzinger contested this comparison, arguing that 'The Council is not called *ekklesia*, but *synedrion*; it does not represent the Church and it *is not* the Church as, on the contrary, any eucharistic celebration is the Church; it is simply a particular service within the Church' (*Catholica* 15 [1961], 292-304, reprinted in *Le nouveau peuple de Dieu,* Paris, Aubier, 1971, p. 88). This leads him to say that coming together as a conciliar gathering is but one way among many of governing the Church. We shall return to this link between Eucharist and synodality.

11. Joseph Ratzinger/Hans Maier, *Démocratisation dans l'Église? Possibilités, limites, risques,* Paris, Apostolat des éditions, 1972, p. 50-51.
12. See in particular Michel Dortel-Claudot, 'L'évêque et la synodalité dans le nouveau Code de droit canonique', *NRT* 106 (1984), p. 641-657. See too B. Franck, who considers synodality to be 'a constitutive reality of the Church' (B. Frank, 'Les expériences synodales après Vatican II', *Communio* III/3 (1978), p. 64). We shall see W. Aymans' differing opinion below.
13. Paolo Ricca, 'Le concile œcuménique. Expression de la collégialité des évêques ou de la "communio ecclesiarum" ou même représentation de toute la communauté des fidèles?', *Concilium* 27 (1983), p. 129-130.
14. André Scrima, 'Simples réflexions d'un orthodoxe sur la constitution', in Guilherme Baraúna and Yves Congar, (eds), *L'Église de Vatican II*, vol. II, Paris, Cerf 1965, p. 1282.
15. Grigorios Larentzakis, 'Die Begründung der Synodalität und der Greminlalität', Pro Oriente, *Konziliarität und Kollegialität als struktur prinzipien der Kirche,* Innsbruck, Tyrola-Verlag, 1975, p. 64.
16. Winfried Aymans, 'Konzil–Bleibendes und Veränderliches im kirchlichen Synodalwesen', in Walter Brandmüller (ed.), *Synodale Strukturen der Kirche. Entwicklung und Probleme*, Donauwörth, Ludwig Auer, 1977, p. 188. Elsewhere Aymans notes that 'while the synodal nature cannot be understood as constitutive of the Church, it is not impossible that synods constitute the bodies of the ordinary direction of the Church.' 'Synodalität Ordentliche oder Ausserordentliche Leitungsform in der Kirche', pro manuscripto, lecture given at the VIIth international canon law conference, Paris, 1990, p.11.
17. See on this Acts 1.15; 11.1; 12.17; 14.2; 21.17-18, etc. On the description of the Church as a brotherhood, see Michel Dujarier, *L'Église-fraternité 1. Les origines de l'expression « adelphotès-fraternitas » aux trois premiers siècles du christianisme*, Paris, Cerf, 1991.

The Synodal Shape of Church Ministry and Order

RICHARD R. GAILLARDETZ

Synodality has become the central theological leitmotif of the Francis Pontificate. It represents a genuine reception and development of the teaching of the Second Vatican Council. Synodality challenges a toxic hierarchology and invites fresh perspectives on public "ordered" ministry in the church, ordained and non-ordained. Finally, the principle of synodality also challenges the current shape of Roman Catholic episcopal governance.

In a speech commemorating the fiftieth anniversary of the establishment of the synod of bishops, perhaps the most consequential speech of his papacy, Pope Francis developed the central theme of his pontificate, synodality. Reflecting on the etymological roots of *synodos*, "journeying together," Francis admitted that synodality was a principle "not so easy to put into practice" yet it "offers us the most appropriate framework for understanding the hierarchical ministry itself."[1] In this essay we will follow the pope's lead and consider from within the horizon of synodality not only "hierarchical ministry" but all public or "ordered" ministries in the church in their relationship with the whole Christian faithful.[2] We begin with a consideration of the gestation of the principle of synodality in the womb of the council's teaching.

Three conciliar teachings figure prominently in the post-conciliar development of the principle of synodality: 1) the church as pilgrim, 2) the whole church as hearer of God's Word, 3) the "co-essential" relationship between baptismal charism and church office.

First, Pope Francis explicitly linked the principle of synodality to the council's theological exploration of the church as pilgrim.[3] This theme was introduced at the council in the very first document it promulgated, the Constitution on the Sacred Liturgy:

"For what marks out the church is that it is at once human and divine, visible and endowed with invisible realities, vigorously active and yet making space in its life for contemplation, present in the world and yet in pilgrimage (*peregrinam*) beyond. . . (SC 2)."[4]

The image highlights a sense of the church's historical embeddedness. Affirming the historicity of the church, in turn, opens up the possibility of authentic reform. Insofar as the church is on pilgrimage, it will always be in need of reform and renewal (UR 6).

Second, synodality evokes a church attentive to God's Word: "A synodal Church is a Church which listens, which realizes that listening is more than simply hearing."[5] Synodality is grounded in the Vatican II's teaching that the church is not a self-contained institution with divine truth as its private possession. Rather, it transcends itself in a posture of openness and receptivity to God's self-disclosure. The whole Christian people are enjoined to listen for God's Word. Participation in the development of tradition is not limited to the magisterium; theologians and all the baptized participate as well (DV 8). The whole Christian faithful are given a supernatural instinct for the faith (*sensus fidei*) that offers them an active role in the life of a "listening" church (LG 12). According to the council, the teaching of the magisterium is less a *determinatio fidei,* an independent determination of the faith of the church, than a *testificatio fidei,* an authoritative witness to that which the bishops have heard.

Finally, synodality draws on the council's teaching that the Holy Spirit bequeaths to the church both charismatic and "hierarchic gifts" (LG 4) that mutually support one another within a non-competitive relationship.[6] As the International Theological Commission (ITC) asserted in its document on synodality, "there also needs to be a decisive promotion of the principle of co-essentiality between hierarchical gifts and charismatic gifts in the Church on the basis of the teaching of Vatican II."[7]

As we can see, the pope's exploration of synodality develops important elements of the teaching of Vatican II even as it provides fresh insight into the ministerial life of the church.

I Synodality, Ministry, and the Critique of Hierarchy

The ITC proposes that synodality is:

> "the specific *modus vivendi et operandi* of the Church, the People of God, which reveals and gives substance to her being as communion when all her members journey together, gather in assembly and take an active part in her evangelizing mission."[8]

How does this "*modus vivendi et operandi*" inform the ministerial life of the church?

Pope Francis regularly speaks of the "hierarchy" and "hierarchical ministries," yet there is an ambiguity embedded in such "hierarchy" language. Insofar as "hierarchy" simply refers to the way in which the church is a sacramentally "ordered" communion, a church built up by both ordained and non-ordained ministries and charisms, the terminology is not necessarily problematic. However, "hierarchy" language has a troubled history that is not so easily overlooked. Yves Congar complained of a "hierarchology" developed over the course of the second millennium: "a wholly pyramidal conception of the Church as a mass totally determined by its summit."[9] Ghislain Lafont has referred to this hierarchological tendency as the "Gregorian form of the church."[10]

When Congar, Lafont and others (including feminist critiques of hierarchy)[11] object to "hierarchy" what they are objecting to is a divinely sanctioned, institutional system comprised of unequal power structures in which a small cadre of persons exercises dominating power over others. This institution is structured pyramidally, with power and the conferral of divine truth being exercised in an exclusively downward vector while ecclesial accountability is exercised in an exclusively upward vector. Those who exercise power are treated as sacral persons and set apart by titles and distinctive garb; as sacral persons they expect uncritical deference from the lay faithful. Following James Keenan, we can speak of "hierarchicalism" as an ecclesiastical culture obsessed with ecclesiastical "grooming" and advancement.[12] This conventional sense of hierarchy has in turn generated and sustained a pernicious, ubiquitous clerical culture.[13]

The principle of synodality can help the church move beyond the abuses of hierarchy, hierarchicalism, and an overarching clerical culture.

In a truly synodal church, a church that learns to "travel together," baptism establishes the most basic ecclesial relation for believers; we are all called to be missionary disciples. To be initiated into the church is to take one's place, one's "*ordo*," within the community, the place of the baptized. As the Orthodox theologian John Zizioulas put it, in a basic sense "there is no such thing as non-ordained persons in the church."[14] To be baptized is to be sacramentally "ordered" within Christ's Body by the power of the Spirit.

If baptism represents the fundamental *ecclesial* ordering of the *Christifideles*, the whole Christian faithful, we can recognize a further *ministerial* ordering, one always at the service of God's people. Those called to ordered ministry never cease belonging to the *Christifideles*; they never lose their basic identity grounded in their baptismal priesthood. As Pope Francis has insisted, "within the Church, no one can be 'raised up' higher than others. On the contrary, in the Church, it is necessary that each person 'lower' himself or herself, so as to serve our brothers and sisters along the way."[15]

Francis subverts the conventional sense of hierarchy as an ascending ladder of rank, power, and privilege, the medieval *cursus honorum*, by re-orienting the pyramidal structure. He invites us to re-imagine the church as "an inverted pyramid" in which "the top is located beneath the base. Consequently, those who exercise authority are called 'ministers' because, in the original meaning of the word, they are the least of all."[16]

A crucial antidote to the dysfunctions and abuses associated with hierarchy, hierarchicalism, and its attendant clerical culture lies in a more adequate account of holy orders informed by the principle of synodality. Such an account will challenge a reductive and warped theology of ordination as the conferral of power and the imposition of a hyper-interiorized, sacramental "character" on the ordinand.[17] A more adequate theology will acknowledge the essential place of the ordained in the life of the church. Ordination effects a distinctive sacramental re-configuration of the *ordinandi* to Christ and his church, but not in an individualistic, hyper-interiorized fashion; ordination effects a fundamental change in ecclesial relationship. It is less about the conferral of power than it is about "an ecclesial re-positioning" that places one within a new ecclesial relationship to Christ and his Body.[18] Appropriate ecclesial accountability, ministerial formation, and sacramental empowerment all follow upon this ecclesial re-positioning. In sacramental ordination the *ordinandi* are not transformed by way of the transmittal of special powers; they are changed by being drawn into a new relationship with Christ and his church. Consequently, sacramental empowerment does not *precede* but rather *follows* upon ordination into a new ecclesial relationship.

One can recognize an analogous ecclesial re-positioning in play when a member of the baptized is called into a new lay ecclesial ministry (e.g., a lector, catechist, pastoral associate) as well. Whether we speak of ordained ministries or the many other ministries exercised by the lay faithful, all such ministries must be re-conceived as distinct, public ministerial relations marked by service to God's people rather than as self-contained offices marked by powers, titles, and privileges.

II The Need for Reform

There is, we must admit, a substantial gap between this synodal vision of ministry and the concrete ministerial reality for many in the church. As we saw earlier, synodality requires that ordered ministries not be reduced to the conferral and exercise of power; rather, each ministry emerges from within the life of the whole church and each exists to serve the flourishing of the church in mission. A commitment to synodality demands a wide-ranging set of reforms in every aspect of the church's ministerial life.

2.1 Lay Ecclesial Ministry

Ordered ministry is not limited by sacramental ordination. Throughout the global church we find an impressive diversity of what in the US church are often referred to as. "lay ecclesial ministries."[19] This development, already flourishing in many local churches, challenges the clerical presupposition that only an elite, clerical caste can exercise formal church ministry. These lay ministries have taken strikingly different forms across the centuries and throughout the global church. In *Querida Amazonia* Pope Francis called for further creative development of inculturated lay ministries appropriate to the needs and resources of local churches (QA 93-4). Lay ministry is no mere clerical auxiliary. Rather, lay ministers merit ministerial formation, a liturgical epiclesis/missioning appropriate for any and all public ministries, and just wages when they are undertaken on a professional basis.

2.1 The Diaconate

One of the much-overlooked contributions of the council concerned the restoration of the diaconate as a permanent, stable ministry in the church, one that would be open to *viri probati*, "mature married men." Unfortunately, this ordained ministry, dedicated to service in liturgy, the Word, and charity (LG 29), has been unevenly implemented. The vast majority of permanent deacons are found in North America, although we can find a few global efforts to implement this ministry in more inculturated forms, as with the Diocese of San Cristóbal de las Casas, in Chiapas Mexico.[20] Much work remains to be done in unlocking the ministerial potential of the diaconate as a permanent ministry. Its restoration is a fine example of the synodal impulse to breakdown the rigidly hierarchical ladder for ecclesiastical advancement (*cursus honorum*) that emerged in the middle ages. No longer would ordination to the diaconate signal but a brief ecclesiastical pause on the way to a "higher" office. Well noted in the Pan-Amazonian synod conversations were calls for a more innovative implementation of the diaconate and requests for the ordination of women to the diaconate.[22]

2.3 The Presbyterate

The demands of synodality also require a thorough re-imagination of the ministerial priesthood: its fundamental theological rationale, the processes for recruitment and formation, and the inculturated forms this ministry might acquire.[23] The church must resist the pressure to produce "numbers" in response to a perceived priest shortage and instead focus on recruiting candidates for presbyteral ministry who demonstrate an ability to discern, empower, form and order the many gifts of the baptized in accord with the council's teaching (LG 12, AA 12, PO 9).

For a synodal church in which all "travel together" there is little justification for a program of priestly formation that walls off seminarians in a remote, quasi-monastic setting, far removed from the daily lives and concerns of those they are being ordained to serve. Given the vital linkage between the ministerial priesthood and the faithful's right to the Eucharist, the church must heed calls for creative, new models for the priesthood that can help stem the "de-eucharistizing" of so many local churches. Finally, we can affirm the evangelical value of celibacy even as we resist the tendency in some quarters to elevate priestly celibacy to quasi-doctrinal status.[24]

2.4 The Episcopate

A synodal view of the teaching ministry of the bishops suggests a circularity in the relationship between the bishops and the lay faithful.[25] Dario Vitali has pointed out that in spite of the council's rediscovery of the *sensus fidei* exercised by all the baptized, the failure to embrace the circular relationship between the sense of the faithful and the magisterium has prevented the council's teaching from having any concrete impact.[26] Throughout his pontificate Pope Francis has highlighted the council's teaching on the *sensus fidei* as much more than a passive echo of magisterial teaching (EG 119, 198). He recognizes that the faithful actually contribute something new to the consciousness of the church and their instinct must be carefully attended to by bishops. The proper circularity between episcopal teaching and the *sensus fidei* requires both a reform of current institutional structures (e.g., episcopal and diocesan synods, diocesan and parish pastoral councils) and the development of new structures more capable of facilitating the participation of the whole Christian faithful in processes of ecclesial discernment. Finally, a consideration of the reform of the episcopate must attend to the distinctive role of the bishop in church governance.

III A Synodal View of Church Governance

The mutual and reciprocal relationship that synodality demands between a bishop and his flock extends beyond the question of the church's teaching office to matters of church governance as well. Both Pope Francis and the ITC have invoked, in their reflections on synodality, the medieval principle: *Quod omnes tangit, ab omnibus tractari et approbari debet*, "what affects everyone ought to be discussed and decided by everyone."[27] This principle challenges the clerical paternalism that informs church governance at every level. A clerical paternalism is unlikely to yield to the demands of this principle without a thorough re-consideration of the bishop's structural relationship to his flock.

As currently structured, the episcopate is largely untethered to the local church. Hervé-Marie Legrand has long called our attention to a problematic feature of Vatican II's teaching on the episcopate, a crucial flaw that has inhibited the full realization of the council's broader ecclesial vision.[28] Legrand has identified two competing theologies of the episcopate in council teaching, one grounded in service to the local church, and the other which sees a bishop's membership in the episcopal college as anterior to his ministry to a local church. Unfortunately, the post-conciliar church has focused on the latter ecclesiological tendency. The current structure of the episcopate has dramatically attenuated the bishop's relationship to his local church. Consider that almost 40% of today's bishops—every ordained church diplomat, many Vatican bureaucrats, and every auxiliary bishop—is assigned to a titular see, that is, a diocese that once existed but no longer does today. So, technically, every bishop is ordained to serve a local church, even if that local church has no living members! How can such a custom *not* trivialize the bishop's relationship to his flock?

The bishop's necessary relationship to his flock is further weakened by the custom, made practically universal in the nineteenth century, by which the Vatican appoints bishops to dioceses with minimal input from the local churches themselves. This practice, in spite of the council's teaching to the contrary (cf. LG 27), reinforces the impression that bishops are merely papal proxies. Finally, we must acknowledge the frequent transfer of bishops from one see to another, often as a form of ecclesiastical promotion from seemingly peripheral pastoral appointments to more prestigious ones. All of these features have served to untether the bishop from the local church.

The reform of the episcopate that authentic synodality demands, finds guidance in the practices of the early church. In the first four centuries, the bishop's relationship to his local church was maintained by far more solidaristic bonds than are present today.

One of the most widely shared convictions of early Christianity concerned the right of the local church to participate, either by election or acclamation, in the appointment of their bishop. In one of the earliest texts to include an ordination ritual, the third century text often attributed to Hippolytus of Rome, *The Treatise on the Apostolic Tradition*, we find an insistence that a bishop be chosen by the people.[29] Almost two centuries later, Pope Celestine I (422-32) could still declare: "Let a bishop not be imposed upon the people whom they do not want"[30] and Pope Leo the Great

(440-61) could insist: "He who has to preside over all must be elected by all."[31] This ancient conviction should inspire a fresh consideration of the current practice of episcopal appointment and encourage more explicitly synodal mechanisms (perhaps modeled on structures incorporated in many professed religious communities) for including the faithful in the process of discerning episcopal appointments.

A second way to strengthen the bond between the bishop and his flock and vitiate the power of clericalism would be to adopt the early church's strict prohibition against the conferral of titular sees, that is, the practice of ordaining a bishop and assigning him a pastoral charge of a non-existent church. This would subvert the sense of episcopal ordination as an honorific or ecclesiastical promotion. Episcopal ordination constitutes a call to a specific form of pastoral leadership of a local church, no more, no less.

Finally, we would do well to re-institute, with prudent modifications, the ancient canonical prohibition[32] against the "translation" of a bishop, that is, the transfer of a bishop from one diocese to another. Occasional exceptions to this canon were made in the early church, but they were rare. This prohibition was intended to forestall episcopal careerism and cement the bond that must exist between a bishop and his people.

In these brief reflections we have considered the theological principle of synodality as a creative reception and development of key insights from the teaching of Vatican II. We have explored the ways in which synodality can shine a bright light on the problematic features of hierarchicalism and clericalism in ministerial and governing structures. Finally, we briefly attended to possible reforms that might restore the ministry and governance of the church to their proper place as a service to the building up of the church in mission. The current pontificate's commitment to the establishment of synodality at every level of church life represents an opportunity we should not squander.

Notes

1. Pope Francis, "Speech Commemorating the Fiftieth Anniversary of the Institution of the Synod of Bishops" (October, 2015). Accessed at: http://www.vatican.va/content/francesco/en/speeches/2015/october/documents/papa-francesco_20151017_50-anniversario-sinodo.html .
2. The term "ordered" here denotes all public ministries within the church, both ordained and non-ordained.
3. Richard R. Gaillardetz, *An Unfinished Council: Vatican II, Pope Francis, and the Renewal of Catholicism* (Collegeville, MN: Liturgical Press, 2015), 67-9, 79-89.
4. Translation from Norman P. Tanner, ed., *Decrees of the Ecumenical Councils* (Washington, DC: Georgetown University Press, 1990), II: 820.
5. Pope Francis, "Speech Commemorating . . . ."
6. Gaillardetz, *An Unfinished Council*, 91-113.
7. International Theological Commission, "Synodality in the Life and Mission of the Church," (2018): # 74, accessed on-line at: http://www.vatican.va/roman_curia/congregations/cfaith/cti_documents/rc_cti_20180302_sinodalita_en.html .
8. ITC, "Synodality. . .", 6. Accessed online at: http://www.vatican.va/roman_curia/congregations/cfaith/cti_documents/rc_cti_20180302_sinodalita_en.html.
9. Yves Congar, "Reception as an Ecclesiological Reality,' *Concilium* 77 (1972): 43-68, at 60. See also his *Lay People in the Church: A Study for a Theology of Laity* (2nd revised edition, Westminster, MD: Newman Press, 1965): 45 and *Power and Poverty in the Church* (Baltimore, MD: Helicon Press, 1964), 70.
10. Ghislain Lafont, *Imagining the Catholic Church: Structured Communion in the Spirit* (Collegeville, MN: Liturgical Press, 2000), 37-64.
11. For two now classic feminist critiques of hierarchy, see Rosemary Radford Ruether, *Women-Church: Theology and Practice of Feminist Liturgical Communities* (San Francisco: Harper & Row, 1985); Elisabeth Schüssler Fiorenza, *Discipleship of Equals: a Critical Feminist Ekklesia-logy of Liberation* (New York: Crossroad, 1993); idem, *The Power of the Word: Scripture and the Rhetoric of Empire* (Minneapolis: Fortress, 2007); v Mary E.
12. James F. Keenan, "Vulnerability and Hierarchicalism," *Melita Theologica* 68/2 (2018): 129-42.
13. See Pope Francis, "Letter to the People of God," (2018), accessed on-line at: http://w2.vatican.va/content/francesco/en/letters/2018/documents/papa-francesco_20180820_lettera-popolo-didio.html .
14. John D. Zizioulas, *Being as Communion* (Crestwood: St. Vladimir's Seminary Press, 1985), 215-6.
15. Pope Francis, "Speech Commemorating . . ."
16. Pope Francis, "Speech Commemorating . . ."
17. Hervé-Marie Legrand, "The 'Indelible' Character and the Theology of Ministry," *Concilium* (1972): 54-62
18. Gaillardetz, "The Ecclesiological Foundations of Ministry . . . ," 36-41.
19. USCCB, *Co-Workers in the Vineyard of the Lord: A Resource for Guiding the Development of Lay Ecclesial Ministry* (Washington, DC: USCCB, 2005). The document can be accessed on-line at: http://www.usccb.org/upload/co-workers-vineyard-lay-

ecclesial-ministry-2005.pdf .
20. See Richard R. Gaillardetz, "Accountability in the Church: Report from Chiapas," *New Theology Review* 19 (2006): 33-45.
21. Phyllis Zagano, *Women: Icons of Christ* (New York, NY: Paulist Press, 2019).
22. See Boston College Priesthood Seminar, "To Serve the People of God: Renewing the Conversation on Priesthood and Ministry," *Origins* 48:31 (December 27, 2018): 484-93.
23. See Cardinal Robert Sarah, and Pope Benedict XVI, *From the Depths of Our Hearts: Priesthood, Celibacy, and the Crisis of the Catholic Church* (San Francisco: Ignatius Press, 2020).
24. ITC, "Synodality . . . ," # 106.
25. Dario Vitali, "The Circularity between *Sensus Fidei* and Magisterium as a Criterion for the Exercise of Synodality in the Church," in *For a Missionary Reform of the Church*, edited by Antonio Spadaro SJ and Carlos María Galli (New York: Paulist, 2017), 196-217.
26. See Pope Francis, "Speech Commemorating . . ." and ITC, "Synodality . . . ," # 65.
27. Hervé-Marie Legrand, "Collégialité des évêques et communion des églises dans la réception de Vatican II," *Revue des Sciences philosophiques et théologiques* 75 (1991): 545-68, and more recently in "*Communio Ecclesiae, Communio Ecclesiarum, Collegium Episcoporum*," in *For a Missionary Reform of the Church*, 159-195.
28. Hippolytus of Rome, *The Treatise on the Apostolic Tradition*, ed. By Gregory Dix and Henry Chadwick (London: Alban Press, 1992).
29. PL, 50:434.
30. PL 54: 634.
31. See Canon 1

Waiting for a 'Copernican Revolution': Ecclesiological Reflections Between Theology and Law

CARLOS SCHICKENDANTZ

Vatican II sketched out a so-called 'Copernican revolution' in the Church's self-understanding. The article gives examples that reveal the procedures operating in recent decades, expose the underlying mentality and demonstrate the systemic problem that indicates that this transformation, to a large extent, has yet to take place. The debate is now in a new context: it has lost its 'innocence' since the enormous potential for abuse in the institutional model under analysis is plain for all to see.

Referring to the Vatican II Constitution on the Church, *Lumen Gentium*, at a *Concilium* congress in 1970, the Belgian cardinal Leo Suenens said: 'It has been said that by changing the order of the chapters so that what was envisaged as third became second, that is, by dealing first with the whole of the Church as the people of God and subsequently with the hierarchy as a service to that people, we carried out a *Copernican revolution*. I think that is true: that change forces us to make a constant mental revolution, the consequences of which we have not yet finished assessing.'[1] The term 'Copernican revolution' was used in the post-conciliar period to describe a radical transformation in the Church's view of itself as compared with an almost thousand-year theological and cultural model of the Church that filtered down into all descriptions of Church life.

The importance of the Gregorian reform (11th century), whose 'central principle' was 'the increase in power of papal authority', cannot be underestimated. It is the great dividing line in the history of the Western

Church'.[2] At least 'in its essential structures', Gislain Lafont argues, the 'Gregorian form' of the Church 'was never abandoned', although it has 'subsequent modifications'.[3] Avery Dulles emphasises an important later moment: 'The current structures of the Church, especially in Roman Catholicism, have a very strong imprint of the past social structures of Western European society,'[4] in other words, 'in practice there remains a mode of government inherited from the European monarchies of the XVIIIth century.'[5]

Hermann Pottmeyer has characterised this inherited hierarchical-monarchical model in terms of five 'priorities': priority of the universal Church over the local churches, of ministers over the community, of the monarchical structure of the ministry over the collegial structure, of ministry over charisms and, finally, the priority of unity over diversity.[6] In the second half of the 20th century, and especially with Vatican II, this model, in each of these priorities, has undergone a radical revision. It is this historical and theological framework briefly sketched out here, that is the context for the 'Copernican revolution'. What it means is the idea of the people of God that stresses the equal dignity of all the sons and daughters of God and emphasises the common membership of the Church community before any distinction of condition or function, ministry charism or service. It is clear that this new self-understanding has a long way to go, and what Suenens called 'a sort of constant mental revolution' is needed if the theory and organisational practices of such a deep-rooted and influential model are to be revised.

Alongside this 'mental revolution' we need a corresponding 'institutional revolution'. In this context an important aspect is the relationship between theology and law, particularly in view of the many inadequacies apparent in the 1983 Code as regards its main claim, namely, to be a translation into canon law of the Council's teachings about the Church.

In the rest of this article I shall offer some examples that reveal they way things have been done in recent decades, display the mentality at work and demonstrate the systemic problem that indicates that the 'Copernican revolution' is still to a large extent unfinished business.

I Three procedural examples

1.1 The Diocesan Pastoral Council

The Diocesan Pastoral Council is a new institution created by the Council which, strictly, has no precedent in the history of the Church. Motivated by the complexity of the diocesan apostolate, the proposal to establish it appeared as early as the preparatory phase of Vatican II, initially with more modest aims, but as the Council went on its nature became clearer, also as a result of the ecclesiological debates, as an instrument to shape all the pastoral activity of a local church. 'It is greatly [to be] desired that in each diocese a pastoral commission will be established over which the diocesan bishop himself will preside and in which specially chosen clergy, religious and lay people will participate' (*Christus Dominus*, 27). Vatican II describes its purpose with three verbs which emphasise analysis, discernment and projection of pastoral activity: 'The duty of this commission will be to investigate and weigh pastoral undertakings and to formulate practical conclusions regarding them' (CD 27). Although the commission responsible for the text maintained that the establishment of this commission 'should be really recommended', it stated that its establishment was not mandatory, and that it depended on the bishop, who headed it, to decide whether it should be consultative or not (AS IV, II, 577). *Christus Dominus*, then, does not require its establishment, but does say that it is 'greatly to be desired' (*valde optandum est)*'.[7]

The Motu Proprio *Ecclesiae Sanctae* (1966) quoted the phrase 'highly recommended' (*valde commendatum*) and asserted that this body 'has a consultative vote only' (16.2). The 1971 synod of bishops phrased the desirability even more strongly, if that were possible: '*magis desiderandum*', 'more to be desired' (AAS 63 1971, 921). In contrast, the current Code of Canon Law (1983) has a very different tone: 'In every diocese and to the extent that pastoral circumstances suggest it, a pastoral council is to be constituted' (Canon 511). In this formulation both recommendation of the establishment of a council and the accompanying positive qualifications 'highly' and 'greatly to be desired' have disappeared. It is very weak language in comparison with all the earlier documentation. In the 2004 Directory for the Pastoral Ministry of Bishops, which recalls that the bishop is not 'bound to do so by canonical discipline' we find a similarly weak expression: 'Ideally, every diocese should establish a diocesan pastoral council.' This weak phrase contrasts with the importance of the role attributed to it: 'expressing through this institution the participation of all the faithful, of whatever canonical state, in the Church's mission' (*Apostolorum succesores*, 184).

In this context, the more recent assertion of the International Theological Commission represents a later strengthening: 'Given its nature, the frequency of its meetings, its procedure and the objectives to which it is committed, the Diocesan Pastoral Council is proposed as *the most appropriate permanent structure for implementing synodality in the local Church*.'[8] This brief historical reference to a body created by the Council is like a metaphor for the emphasis in ecclesiology and the procedures in last few decades: (a) it shows a contradictory development, and in the case of the Code of Canon Law a significant regression; (b) the asset that is being protected is explicitly mentioned, the bishop's freedom to establish a council or not, which makes it optional; (c) there is an increasing recourse to lofty theological rhetoric, 'participation' and 'synodality', without a corresponding organisational and juridical translation; (d) the possible deliberative character seems to be dismissed as early as the beginning of the post-conciliar period, though this outcome does not seem to be implied in Vatican II's more open teaching.

Another piece of current information is relevant. A recent Australian report shows that two-thirds of Australian dioceses lack this permanent structure. Almost certainly the situation in Australia is not an exception in the Church.[9] Fifty-five years after Vatican II, no 'Copernican revolution'!

1.2 Presbyteral Council

In the case of the Presbyteral Council, rather than create a new body, the Council clearly manifested the idea of renewing the cathedral chapters and the college of consultors, both in existence at that time (*Presbyterorum ordinis*, 7). The doubts expressed by some Council fathers about the ambiguous nature of the terms 'senate' and of 'priests representing all the priests' were tempered by the cautious description of its function: 'This representative body by its advice (*suis consiliis*) will be able to give the bishop effective assistance in the administration of the diocese' (PO 7). The theological and historical arguments that supported its establishment, however, left open the space for deciding the specific form of the 'assistance', and was not precise in its legal form. The rules, from as far back as the document *Ecclesiae sanctae* of 1966, provided that its opinion was consultative and, according to the 1983 Code of Canon Law, oblige the bishop to seek its opinion in seven precisely defined cases.[10] But there was also a provision that 'the diocesan bishop is to hear it in affairs of greater importance but needs its consent only in cases expressly defined by law' (Canon 500,2). But the law has not specified any case! Decades later one is surprised by the lack of initiative or creativity in failing to create a more incisive possibility of participation that is already provided for in the canonical system – the deliberative character of a council.

This particular situation, which is so obvious, reflects the general tendency to guarantee the 'freedom' of authorities without paying sufficient attention to participation, even, as in this case, that of the bishop's closest collaborators, in discernment and decision-making. The technical expression generally used in these contexts runs: 'while always maintaining the power of the bishops themselves to act freely' (*Ecclesiae Sanctae*, introduction). Encouraged by a particular ecclesiological mentality, current law shows itself scrupulous – in not linking episcopal authority to processes of discernment and consensus-building.

1.3 Prior investigation in abuse cases

A third example concerns abuses against minors and one of the most frequently made mistakes in the process of reporting in a wide range of countries. It is a feature common to many proposals from bishops conferences, dioceses and religious congregations that reflects an important systemic weakness protected by current canon law. I shall take as an example a specific text. The *Charter for the Protection of Children and Young People* of the US Conference of Catholic Bishops, revised in 2011, despite its many important aspects, has one important gap. While it provides for the creation of 'a review board which will function as a confidential consultative body to the bishop/eparch in discharging his responsibilities' (*Essential Norms*, 4), it does not specify the absolute need for obligatory consultation of this board when one person, the bishop or eparch, decides whether there is a reasonable belief or 'sufficient evidence' that abuse has occurred in order to continue the investigation (*Essential Norms*, 6). The

US *Charter*, understandably, is not an exception in this point: a review of the episcopal documents from Ireland, Canada, Australia, Chile, Mexico, Argentina, etc., will show the same procedure. Neither canon law (Canon 1717,1) nor the 2011 circular from the Congregation for the Doctrine of the Faith, *Circular Letter to Assist Episcopal Conferences in Developing Guidelines for Dealing with Cases of Sexual Abuses of Minors Perpetrated by Clerics*, require anything else.[11]

In this area, this is situation that can be observed today: review committees or bodies to advise bishops, dioceses and religious congregations, but there is no guarantee, even in law, that they *must* be consulted. This reveals one of the most common, and at the same time most basic, systemic dysfunctions in the Catholic Church's current theological and cultural model, the discretionary nature of the exercise of authority. No individual – bishop, eparch, religious superior – should be able to make a decision of this sort without a legally binding provision that guarantees that as independent as possible a committee is consulted to make a correct decision more likely. It would seem that people do not learn from their own mistakes, even from one of the most common: bishops and religious superiors in the most diverse countries made the mistake, protected by canon law, which did not require it, of not initiating or not halting investigations without institutionally backed advisory procedures, and did not have to answer for their decision to any authority, personal or institutional.

Pope Francis' *motu proprio* of May 2019, *Vos Estis Lux Mundi*, is a text that has generally been seen in a positive light. It refers only to complaints of abuse by bishops or those in similar positions – who are directly under the authority of the Pope. It imposes an obligation to report, protects those who have given evidence, requires the creation of bodies for listening to complaints in every diocese, etc. But it does not deem to modify the precise point under discussion here, that is, it does not include a modification of Canon 1717, 1. The inclusion of laypeople in the advisory process is optional, as is consulting them. This document can be said to reflect a greater accountability, in comparison with the previous situation, but only in one direction, to the Pope, but not in relation to the communities over which the bishop presides.

1.4 What do these three cases have in common?

The common feature, expressed in different ways, is not linking Church authority to any other institutional or personal authority belonging to the communities they lead. They make clear that if a process of consultation takes place, it is solely by the goodwill of the person who presides. Only in the case of the presbyteral council is a consultative opinion demanded in a few precisely defined situations, but the deliberative character, proposed as possible, is made a nonsense in practice by the lawgiver: no case is stipulated. The arguments of some of the main international reports on the abuse of minors, such as those from Australia or Germany, which refer to the specific risk within the Catholic Church, namely clerical power, are proved to the letter here: there is no appropriate system of accountability. The authorities don't have to answer for their actions; they are not required to share information, consultation with specialists in various fields and the most basic participation of the people of God is left to the whim of the person in charge. The pastor may 'smell of the sheep', but his system of government, in contrast, has the typical features of authoritarianism. We need a form of accountability, not only to Rome, such as the Vatican is now feebly attempting to introduce, but also to their peers and, above all, to the communities they legitimately govern.

What was one of the central points of the 'Copernican revolution'? That the ordained minister is not 'above', but first and foremost 'one with' the people of God; his task of presiding is located within the Church communities of which he forms part.

This more horizontal relationship, rooted in law, should not be thought of merely as a limitation of episcopal authority, but as a different way of exercising that authority. Theologically it can be imagined as a closer bond with the Spirit through a closer bond with the protagonists of the people of God, since 'to each is given the manifestation of the Spirit for the common good' (1 Cor 12.7). In addition, it also encourages the building up of a community, the building of consensus that ensures that the decisions taken are better received and so allow for a more rapid and better implementation of what has been decided in common.

II Two existing starting-points

The Code of Canon Law itself has two helpful precedents that have not been used. If in the economic sphere it is recognised that in specific cases the bishop needs the agreement of other people to take a decision (Canon 1277), this means that the possibility of a deliberative vote cannot be vaguely identified with the improper introduction of a practice from parliamentary democracy, as some people fear. 'A superior needs the consent or counsel of some college or group of persons,' for their action to be valid in law is already a principle in current canon law (Canon 127). Accordingly, if we bear in mind the principle stated in Canon 127 and what is said in Canon 129 about the possibility of delegating the power of governance (*sacra potestas*) to laypeople,[12] it can be seen that developing a greater structural synodality already has almost decisive precedents. We can leave open the theological question that has been a matter of debate, whether the lay faithful 'participate' or only 'cooperate' in the power of governance; that is something that needs to be explored and defined more precisely by theology. Whatever the case, the lawgiver finally chose the latter, weaker position. It should be noted that the 'cooperation' was stated deliberately, against the opinions of well-known people who advised that it should be excluded, and any sort of power of governance should be denied to laypeople. In fact, the Code of Canon Law gives authority for this in various cases, judges, defenders of the bond, auditors, lawyers, finance directors in dioceses and parishes, superiors and council members in institutes of consecrated life or societies of apostolic life.[13] Accordingly, it is clear that under current law the Church has the authority to admit lay men and women to posts and responsibilities that imply the exercise of the power of governance, that is, the public power necessary to perform validly a juridical act (legislative, executive or judicial) that results in a decision binding on Church life. The various historical experiences and canon law itself suggest that: 'It is clear that, in the discussion about who can exercise the power of governance, we are not in the sphere of immutable divine law, but in merely ecclesiastical law, which can change, has changed, and it is very probably that there will be further developments.'[14] Such 'cooperation' in governance, already stated, is enough to allow for important steps in a comprehensive synodal reform of the Code of Canon Law.

III A new context: abuses of power, of conscience and sexual

The debate is now in a new context: it has lost its 'innocence', since it is plain for all to see that there is enormous potential for abuse intrinsically rooted in the form of governance we are analysing.

The various international studies are trying to identify the specific feature of this institution, the Catholic Church, that makes it different from educational or sporting establishments where abuses have been found. If we accept the diagnosis of the 'systemic nature' of the problem, we are trying to identify, in the words of the German study, 'the structural characteristics' of the Catholic Church 'that encourage the sexual abuse or minors or make preventing it difficult', its 'specific risk.[15] The same document, in a similar way to other reports and theological reform agendas, has no doubt where an essential factor lies: 'Sexual abuse always represents also an abuse of power, and this can be facilitated by the authoritarian and clerical structures of the Catholic Church.' It therefore calls for a 'change in the structures of clerical power', in other words, 'a fundamental examination of the ordained ministry of the priest and of the understanding of his role as regards non-ordained people'. And it warns clearly: verbal recognition, punishment of individuals, the payment of financial compensation and the drawing up of prevention measures are necessary, 'but they are in no sense adequate measures'. If the Church's responses are limited to such measures, these regulations, positive in themselves, could turn out to be favourable 'to the preservation of clerical power, since *they only identify the symptoms* of an undesirable development and therefore prevent a debate about *the fundamental problem* raised by clerical power'.[16] The Copernican revolution is not now being proposed by bishops and theologians, as at Vatican II, but demanded by psychologists, psychiatrists, lawyers and, above all, by victims.

Translated by Francis McDonagh

Notes

1. Léon-Joseph Suenens, "Algunas tareas teológicas de la hora actual", *Concilium* extra (1970) 183-193, 185 .
2. John W. O'Malley, 'La reforma en la vida de la Iglesia', in: Antonio Spadaro and Carlos María Galli (ed), *La reforma y las reformas en la Iglesia*, Maliaño, 2016, pp 97-120, quotation from p. 101.
3. Ghislain Lafont, *Imagining the Catholic Church*, Collegeville, MN, 2000, p. 37.
4. Avery Dulles, *Models of the Church*, New York, 5th ed., 2002, p. 191.
5. Hervé Legrand, 'Quelques réflexions ecclésiologiques sur l'Histoire du concile Vatican II', *Revue des sciences philosophiques et théologiques* 90 (2006), 495-520, quotation from p. 516.
6. Cf. Hermann Pottmeyer, *Die Rolle des Papsttums im Dritten Jahrtausend*, Freiburg im Breisgau, 1999, p. 121.
7. Cf. Serena Noceti, 'Christus Dominus. Commento', in: Erio Castellucci et al., *Commentario ai documenti del Vaticano II*, Vol. 4, Bologna, 2017, pp 43-189, quotation from p. 130.
8. International Theological Commission, *Synodality in the Life and Mission of the Church*, March 2018, 81: http://www.vatican.va/roman_curia/congregations/cfaith/cti_documents/rc_cti_20180302_sinodalita_en.html (italics added).
9. Cf. 'The Light from the Southern Cross', 104, https://www.ncronline.org/sites/default/files/file_attachments/03-FINAL-Southern-Cross-Report-010520-SinglePage_1.pdf
10. Cf. Canons 461 § 1, 515 § 2, 531, 536 § 1, 1215 § 2, 1222 § 2 and 1263.
11. http://www.vatican.va/roman_curia/congregations/cfaith/documents/rc_con_cfaith_doc_20110503_abuso-minori_en.html
12. Canon 129, 2: 'Lay members of the Christian faithful can cooperate in the exercise of this same power according to the norm of law.'
13. Cf John Beal, 'The Exercise of the Power of Governance by Lay People', *The Jurist* 55 (1995) 1-92, 52-88.
14. John Huels, 'The Power of Governance and its Exercise by Lay Persons', *Studia canonica* 35 (2001) 59-96, quotation from p. 72. Translated from the Spanish.
15. *Sexueller Missbrauch an Minderjährigen durch katholische Priester, Diakone und männliche Ordensangehörige im Bereich der Deutschen Bischofskonferenz*, September 2018, p.15. See https://dbk.de/themen/sexueller-missbrauch/
16. *Sexueller Missbrauch*, pp 17, 18 (italics added).

Synodality is a Matter of Practice: A Plea for Learning

HERVÉ LEGRAND OP

Authoritarian clerical ecclesiology inherited from the long 19th century is in a systemic crisis. Theologians believe, as does Pope Francis, that the rise of synodality will provide a remedy. The abuse scandal has made its inadequacies plain to all, though changes in society had already made them painfully obvious. This article explores a series of learning experiences that would allow lay people to exercise their citizenship in the Church by means of various councils that are part of the structures, and diocesan synods, within which clergy have their proper place. Their vocation and their ordination place them in the Church and not simply over against it by an erroneous quasi-assimilation to Christ and powers that they can supposedly exercise as they see fit.

In his address commemorating the 50th anniversary of the institution of the synod of bishops, Pope Francis described synodality as 'precisely this path which God expects of the Church of the third millennium'. He added just afterwards: 'What the Lord is asking of us is already in some sense present in the very word "synod". Journeying together — laity, pastors, the Bishop of Rome — is an easy concept to put into words, but not so easy to put into practice.'[1] Since then the issue has no longer been to explore further the theological foundations of synodality or its pastoral relevance, but to put it into practice.

Talking about it is not enough. After Vatican II all the talk in favour of collegiality produced no more than a meagre result, recorded in *Apostolos suos*.[2] 'Affective collegiality' was prized more than 'effective collegiality', which was only to be found in an ecumenical council.[3] The same thing could happen to synodality if there is no effort to bring it to life in what is a particularly propitious moment, as it is required by the current situation, pastorally and doctrinally.

I A particularly good time to push for synodality

As regards the situation, the request for synodality owes much to the scale of sexual offences committed by clergy (including high-ranking clergy) and, perhaps even more, to the clear inertia of the bishops, or the Holy See, who have covered up for the guilty. Such a failure is, in the strict sense, structural. The origin can be found in current ecclesiology, which has remained clerical and authoritarian, despite the last Council. We are facing a crisis of the system that cannot be dealt with by spiritual exhortations, desirable as these may be; it will last as long as the shared responsibility of all and some within the people of God has not become a reality, at local and diocesan level and more widely.

Pastorally, the clerical and authoritarian ecclesiology that was kept in place beyond Vatican II was already exhausted as a result of the profound social changes that took place from the middle of the 20th century, especially in the West. Until then priests were locked into a clergy-laity binary in which the roles were clearly defined: the clergy governed, taught and celebrated for the benefit of laity, who were governed, taught and who attended the clergy's celebrations,[4] in accordance with the papal teaching common between 1890 and 1950.[5] What was viable at the time, in mainly rural, simple and largely uneducated societies, proved dysfunctional in societies that are more and more urbanised, bombarded with information, complex and innovatory, and which encourage the emancipation of individuals and especially of women. But not everyone realised this, since John Paul II's revised Code of Canon Law made few corrections to the 1917 version.[6]

Doctrinally, there is a now a broad consensus that synodal or conciliar life is part of the very essence of the Church.[7] This issue of *Concilium* provides enough evidence for this to show that its doctrinal identity is at risk when synodality dozes off. Vatican II's *Lumen Gentium* begins, rightly, by stating that the Church is the people of God the Father, the body of Christ and the temple of the Holy Spirit.[8] If it is the temple of the Holy Spirit, this means that the whole range of the gifts of the Spirit, in their diversity, can only be found in the whole of the people of God, and since no one Christian, and no one Church, has a monopoly of these, that implies a system of listening to each other and co-responsibility. In the same way, if the Church is the body of Christ, with a great diversity of members, as St Paul insists, all are called to collaborate in unity. That is why the people of God is called *ecclesia* (which gives us our family of 'ecclesial' words), or 'assembly'. This shows how much the revival of synodality is justified doctrinally.

Make a start on the learning required to intensify synodal life

The various attempts at resistance to synodal possibilities, noted by Pope Francis, will not be overcome by longer doctrinal arguments, or by decrees. We will get there through learning experiences, made necessary by the enormous loss of credibility suffered by the clerical system. Priests, bishops and faithful have experienced the mistakes of the doctrinal and canonical common places that nurtured clericalism. The clergy are discovering the need to promote synodality and find that they have some resources to do so. Many of the baptised are taking seriously their responsibility as citizens in the Church and everyone realises that they are embarking on a learning process that requires institutional creativity and will take time. The next sections will explore these two perspectives for learning to live a more synodal life.

II Pastors have an important role to play in developing the reciprocal links that connect them with the faithful.

2.1 Pastors are best placed to encourage more synodality

For synodality to become a reality, we have of course to 'fight clericalism'. But such a slogan is dangerous. Denouncing the clerical system may lead us to include in it, unjustly, all priests; far from all being clerical, they too are victims of a system they want to correct. They have an ability to reset the system to advance synodality. Apart from their personal attitudes, which are important, they can influence underlying questions such as the privilege given in Catholicism to ministers as opposed to the object of their ministry and the attitudes encouraged by an overestimate of the effects of ordination.[9] This is perfectly possible in the present situation, while we wait for future structural reforms.

2.2 Pastors can contribute to correcting the Catholic tendency to emphasise the person of the ministers over the object of their ministry. *A local diagnosis* Whereas ordination is first and foremost a grace for the Church, it is generally presented first and foremost as a special grace for the person of the priest.[10] This can be seen from the divergence in the French translations of Eph 4.11-12, which talks about ministers. The liturgical Lectionary and the *Traduction Oecuménique de la Bible* translate this passage accurately: 'Christ gave some as apostles, others as prophets or evangelists, or pastors and teachers, to enable the saints to carry out the ministry to build up the body of Christ.' But five French-language Catholic bibles (Crampon, Liénart, Maredsous, Osty, Bible de Jérusalem) give an identically incorrect translation: 'Christ gave *to some* the gift *of being* apostles, *to others* the gift *of being* prophets, etc.' Whereas Paul says nothing about the nature of these ministers, nor of any gift given to them, because it is they who are given to others for the common task of building, these translations focus the ministers on themselves and their ontology, revealing a denominational prejudice[11] hardly welcoming to synodality.[12]

Resetting the theology of vocation to the ministry A vocation to the priesthood is still commonly thought of as a personal appeal received from Christ after an interior spiritual process. 'He has a vocation,' people say of a person, and they go on to say: 'He's become a priest,' in accordance with canon law, which constantly calls him 'the candidate',[13] and obliges him to ask for his ordination in writing from the bishop of the diocese he himself has chosen to join.[14] In addition, through the sacrifice represented by celibacy, he will be sharply distinguished from the common human condition. The result for priests is a an exclusively high level of complementarity as regards the faithful, which does little to encourage synodality. Doctrinally this obliterates the formal criterion of vocation, the choice of the Church.[15] In practice, we are forced to exclude some candidates and refrain from appealing to others who would be suitable. Finally, from lack of candidates, there will be no more priests. According to the Directory (18), the only solution is to pray for vocations.

Pastors can help to rectify such a theology. In many French dioceses and even in Rome, instead of waiting for candidates for the permanent diaconate, people have approached them on the witness of other Christians and priests who know them. They had not felt called and were not volunteers. They assented to the Church's call and the bishop ordained them. In this way we have acquired experience of being able to call a number of *viri probati* to the presbyterate, where the needs of the ministry are regarded as more important than the state of life of the ministers.

2.3 Pastors can also correct, a little more than at the edges, the understanding of the effects of ordination that places priests only over against the Church, in a position of power and quasi-assimilation to Christ himself.

When official or unofficial documents such as the Code of Canon Law, the Catechism of the Catholic Church and the Directory on Popular Piety and the Liturgy, twenty or thirty years after Vatican II, present the effects of ordination, they ignore the doctrinal adjustment made by *Lumen Gentium* when it discussed the people of God before talking about the ministers within it.[16] According to the Catechism, as for the Code of Canon Law and the Directory,[17] the first effect of ordination is the conferring of a 'sacred power to act in the person of Christ the Head',[18] on a Christian who will later receive a pastoral charge. In addition, these texts talk about the indelible character of *priesthood*; in other words, they systematically describe the priest as *sacerdos* and not *presbyter*, as *Presbyterorum Ordinis* had wanted.[19] This breaks up the *tria munera* to the detriment of pastoral ministry and the ministry of the Word. This priesthood is said to be different 'in essence, and not in degree, from the common priesthood', without making it clear that this difference is not an ontological difference between priests and lay people.[20] Detached from pastoral ministry, this power becomes a personal attribute, which creates serious doctrinal problems, notably as regards the eucharist[21] and the apostolic succession.[22] Worse, according to law, a bishop or priest, even if dismissed or apostate, can celebrate mass and ordain validly if they have the intention of doing what the Church does.[23] Finally, ordination is said to increase sanctifying grace and confer a new relationship to the Trinity,[24] ontologically transforming the ordained person to the point of making him 'another Christ', if not 'Christ himself'.[25]

Why then should it be a surprise that the Code of Canon Law describes the start of a parish priest's ministry as 'taking possession' and that the Directory ends with a reference to the solitude of the priest?

2.4 Pastors can correct a conception of ordination that places ordained ministers above the Church or detached from it.

At an ordination, using the rite, a bishop can easily ensure that the request for ordination comes from a member of the assembly and not from the ordinand himself, and emphasise the testimony of other Christians. He can also place the ordinand's profession of faith in this framework, so that when one of their members enters the apostolic ministry all realise that they are its guardians along with him. Similarly, in the case of a priest, the bishop could mention the specific community that is to receive him.

Neither synods nor pastoral councils are obligatory, but by calling meetings regularly and reporting to them, a bishop would be the first to show that the ministers are part of the *ecclesia*. Within these two bodies, and within the council of presbyters, he could also ask, via a secret ballot for the names of candidates for the episcopate.[26] In the right conditions, parochial pastoral councils are places for forming connections between pastors and faithful, in addition to informal initiatives.

III Familiarising the baptised with their civil rights in the Church by appealing to their civic experience.

Are the Catholic people well informed about synodality? After the sexual and financial scandals revealed by the media, they are demanding reforms, but they do not know how to play an active role in the Church. Now all know that their baptism makes them citizens in the Church.[27] Since they have experience of democracy, it is important to make a clear distinction between democracy and synodality. We can take a synod as an example.

3.1 Diocesan synods follow citizen procedures

Canons 460-468 lay down four 'citizen' procedures which could become familiar if synods were held more frequently. In sum, they are as follows.

Circulation of information Synodal life, like democracy, requires freedom of information. In order to exercise their responsibilities, the members of the synod need to know the human, ministerial and financial resources their Church has available. They also need to learn to manage their relations with the media and social networks, because the Gospel is meant for everyone.

Freedom of expression Free discussion by citizens of matters that concern them is the characteristic feature of democracy. Canon 465 also provides that 'All proposed questions are subject to the free discussion of the members during sessions of the synod.' If information circulates freely in this way, debates will expand the questions and answers and allow for better communication with society, because any debate that is stifled in the Church emerges in the public sphere in the worst possible way.

Negotiation and respect for minorities Better than in democracy, synods take their decisions by consensus, which means over a longer time-frame and with compromises, which better respect those who have difficulty in expressing themselves or who disagree.

Participation in the framing of the laws that govern us As in a democracy, members of the synod vote on the laws they will apply in the framework of particular diocesan law. It is a learning process in Catholicism, but one which is often stifled by universalist legislation.[28]

3.2 Citizenship in synods differs from that in parliaments

The synod model is taken from the Acts of the Apostles, where we can see how a synod balances the responsibility of the whole body and particular groups. In order to re-establish the college of the Twelve, Peter does not act on his own authority. *On his own*, he addresses 'the brothers' (the whole group), and they suggest two people, but neither Peter nor the Eleven choose. They refer the decision to God, by drawing lots (Acts 1.15-26). In Acts 6.1-16 the Twelve do not proceed by 'executive action', but (as a group) they make a proposal 'to the whole community'. It 'pleased the whole community', who selected the Seven (a group), who were entrusted with the ministry, so resolving the conflict.

The present synods have an identical structure. They are presided over by the bishop (*one person*), have statutory members (*a group*), but the overwhelming majority of the assembly are elected (*all*). Neither the bishop nor the synod is sovereign. The texts adopted must be promulgated by the bishop, and he cannot change them or add to them except by a decree outside the synod. In addition, he will not promulgate anything that breaks communion with the rest of the Church, because his Church, while fully the Church, is not the whole Church. This communion ecclesiology should remove the fear that synodality will lead to excesses, especially since a diocesan synod does not pronounce on the content of the faith.

The participation of all includes women, because women Christians speak and vote in synods despite the prohibitions of 1 Cor 14.34 and 1 Tim 2. 11-12 without objections from the most traditional Christians. It is the first step in a successful inculturation process.[29]

3.3 No synodal Church without institutional creativity bringing together canon lawyers and theologians

Vatican II mentions the Church 1,135 times and canon law five times. The lesson to be drawn from this is clear. Synodality will not go from an idea to a reality without institutional creativity that brings canon lawyers and theologians closely together.[30] Diocesan synods, pastoral, diocesan and parish councils are all optional, whereas they are the only bodies to include lay people in any numbers. Could decrees make them obligatory? Learning is still needed here.

If we take the example simply of the diocesan synod, for which there is no general rule, locally it will be necessary:

To determine its *composition*: Who can elect and be elected? What are the criteria of age, sex, geography (proportion of rural/urban members)? What is the status of the experts and invited guests (from other denominations[31])?

To draw up an agenda tailored to the powers of the assembly, together with the necessary background documents;

To establish the working and voting procedures: speaking time, quorums, role of committees, procedures for amendments, settling disputes.

Of course, dioceses will learn from each other in this process.

IV Conclusion

What promise does synodal life hold out? The benefit for all of us, bishops, priests, deacons, religious and Christians in general, is an opportunity to meet, to listen to each other, to work on decision together in the light of the Gospel so that parishes and dioceses can be better witnesses to it. Of course, the voice of the saints and prophets is precious, but for clericalism to fade we need institutional reforms that will create different attitudes through practice.[32]

Finally, we may note that a synodal assembly is a graced event. In the Old Testament God accompanied his people on their journey. Why would he not visit us when we too set out on our synodal journey?

Translated by Francis McDonagh

Notes

1. http://www.vatican.va/content/francesco/en/speeches/2015/october/documents/papa-francesco_20151017_50-anniversario-sinodo.html.
2. For John Paul II in this Apostolic Letter, bishops conferences are creations of the papacy, lacking even an ordinary magisterium. In addition, in asserting that the episcopal college 'is a reality which precedes the office of being the head of a particular Church' (12), he dissociated them from communion between the churches.
3.This language was coined by John-Paul II.
4. The entry 'Lay' in the *Kirchenlexikon* VIII (1891), p.1323, consists merely of 'See *Clergy*'. In it we read that 'No-one can seriously argue for a priesthood of the laity. An attempt to deduce one from 1 Peter 2.5-9 is a sign of exegetical deviance.' And Pius XII also taught that 'as often as a priest repeats what the divine Redeemer did at the Last Supper, the sacrifice is really completed whether the faithful are present…or are not present, since it is in no wise required that the people ratify what the sacred minister has done', Encyclical *Mediator Dei*, 96: http://www.vatican.va/content/pius-xii/en/encyclicals/documents/hf_p-xii_enc_20111947_mediator-dei.html.
5. Repeating Leo XIII, Pius X teaches in *Vehementer nos*: 'The one duty of the multitude is to allow themselves to be led, and, like a docile flock, to follow the Pastors' (8): http://www.vatican.va/content/pius-x/en/encyclicals/documents/hf_p-x_enc_11021906_vehementer-nos.html.
6. The 1917 Code devoted a single general positive canon to the laity, who 'have the right of receiving from the clergy, according to the norm of ecclesiastical discipline, spiritual goods and especially that aid necessary for salvation' (682). After the publication of the 1983 Code, Cardinal Schotte, the secretary general of the synod of bishops, was still able to say: 'Don't make any mistake. In the Catholic Church a parish priest is answerable to no-one except his bishop; a bishop is answerable to no-one except the Pope. And the Pope is answerable to no-one except God,' *The Tablet*, 17 November 2001.
7. For an overall view, see Hervé Legrand, 'La sinodalità al Vaticano II e dopo il Vaticano; un'indagine e una riflessione teologica e istituzionale', ATI, *Chiesa e sinodalità. Coscienza, forme, processi*, Milano, 2007, pp. 67-108.
8. 'Thus, the Church has been seen as "a people made one with the unity of the Father, the Son and the Holy Spirit"'(Vatican II, *Lumen Gentium*,4).
9. Those interested in an overall theology of ordination, may like to see my presentation in 'Initiation à la pratique de la théologie', *Dogmatique* II, Paris, 3rd edition, 1993.
10. For St Thomas Aquinas, the grace of ordination is a grace for someone else, 'to build up the Church', and not for the person ordained: 'Sanctifying grace is not a mark of our orders,' (*Contra Gentiles*, IV, 74; *IV Sent*. dist. XXIV q. 1; art 1, sol. 1, ad 3um, repeated

in Suppl. IIIa pars, q.34, art. 1, ad 3um).

11. See Per Erik Persson, *Representatio Christi. Der Amtsbegriff in der neueren römisch-katholischen Amtstheologie*, Göttingen, 1966. At the Reformation Catholics were kept away from Protestant preaching because 'what is important is not what is said, but who says it.'

12. These translations lead a parish priest automatically to ask parishioners for help instead of asking them: 'What can I do for you so that you and we together can be good servants of the Gospel?'

13. Eleven canons use this term, four have 'aspirants' and three 'destined for orders'.

14. Canon 1016 (incardination) and Canon 1036 (request for ordination). The requirement of an oath sworn on the Gospels that one is certain of having a vocation (*cum experiar ac sentio me esse a Deo revera vocatum*) required by the Congregation of the Sacraments (AAS 23 [1931], 127), has probably fallen into disuse.

15. Pius X explicitly confirmed this doctrine: 'What is called a priestly vocation does not consist, at least necessarily and generally, of some sort of inner attraction or of invitations from the Holy Spirit' (AAS 4 (1912) 485-486).

16. And they don't take account of LG 30: 'Pastors... also know that they were not ordained by Christ to take upon themselves alone the entire salvific mission of the Church toward the world. On the contrary they understand that it is their noble duty to shepherd the faithful and to recognize their ministries and charisms, so that all according to their proper roles may cooperate in this common undertaking with one mind. See also *Presbyterorum Ordinis*, 9: 'Priests must sincerely acknowledge and promote the dignity of the laity and the part proper to them in the mission of the Church...For priests are brothers among brothers with all those who have been reborn at the baptismal font. They are all members of one and the same Body of Christ, the building up of which is required of everyone.'

17. *Catechism*, 1681: effect of ordination, CIC, canon 1008.

18. So in *Catechism* 875, 1538, 1548 ('possesses the authority to act in the power and place of the person of Christ himself [*virtute ac persona ipsius Christi*])' 1552, 1563, and frequently.

19. The *Directory* uses the word sixty times in the sense of John-Paul II's *Pastores dabo vobis*, where priests are called *sacerdotes* three times more often than *presbyteri*.

20. This theological statement has an effect: according to the Survey of American Catholic Priests (1973 1993, 2001), 80% of US priests believe themselves to be ontologically different from lay people.

21. This has led, not just to private masses, but to the recommendation, for the first time in history of solitary celebrations of the sacrament of unity 'for a just and reasonable cause' (Canon 906), a sign of piety, the canon lawyers say. *The Directory on the Ministry and Life of Priests*, 67, uses this canon to support its recommendation that priests should celebrate mass daily. There is an identical recommendation in *Sacramentum Caritatis* 80 (with note 224, the wish of the synod); cf AAS 99 (2007), 167, in both cases with the qualification *etiam fidelisbus ausentibus* ('even if the laity are not present'). Josef Ratzinger regarded this as 'one of the most unfortunate effects of medieval theology' (*Le nouveau peuple de Dieu*, Paris, 1971, ppl 20-121.

22. For protocol and administrative reasons, bishops are ordained without dioceses: Cardinals Brandmüller, Grech et Ries were ordained in this way at the ages of 82, 87 and 92 respectively. Such ordinations are invalid according to Canon 6 of Nicea and Canons 6 and 29 of Chalcedon. They give a false idea of the apostolic succession as something transmitted by the hands of one individual to another (as Mgr Lefebvre believed and as

illustrated by the site www.catholic-hierarcgy.org). In fact, a bishop does not succeed the bishop who ordained him, but the one who preceded him in a see, as all lists of succession show.

23. Cf. C. Vogel, *Ordinations inconsistantes et caractère indélébile*, Turin, 1978, Foreword.

24. This position of the Munich dogmatic theologian Michael Schmaus (*Katholische Dogmatik* IV, 1, Munich, 1957, § 284, 2 a & c) was adopted by *Pastores dabo vobis* 12 c, and by the Directory (2).

25. This expression, rejected at Vatican II (*Acta synodalia*, III, IV, 247), is adopted and expanded by Cardinal Robert Sarah: 'The priest is identified with Christ. He becomes not just alter Christus, another Christ. He is really *ipse Christus*; he is Christ himself', *Des profondeurs de nos cœurs*, Paris, 2020, pp 131-132.

26. The recent dismissal of four cardinals shows that the selection of bishops would benefit if opinions were sought from Christians.

27. The Code of Canon Law in force until 1983 gave the laity no more than 'the rights accorded by states to foreign citizens with residence or protected status.' See U. Stutz, *Der Geist des Codex iuris canonici*, Stuttgart, 1918, pp. 83-88.

28. Recently the Roman Curia issued universal rules on girl altar servers and imposed inappropriate linguistic corrections on liturgical translations approved by local episcopates.

29. And it will continue. On the conditions required for women's ordination, see Hervé Legrand, 'La fraternité chrétienne, dépassement de la hiérarchisation entre femmes et hommes dans l'Église', in: M. Camdessus (ed.), *Transformer l'Eglise à la lumière de Fratelli tutti*, Paris, 2020, pp. 159-172.

30. On this necessary, if difficult, collaboration, see Hervé Legrand, 'Les enjeux ecclésiologiques de la codification du droit canonique. Quelques réflexions sur la portée de l'option choisie en 1917', in: P. Parabeyre and B. Basdevant-Gaudemet (ed.), *Les clercs et les princes. Doctrines et pratiques de l'autorité ecclésiastique à l'époque moderne* (*Etudes et rencontres de l'Ecole des Chartes* 41), Paris, 2013, pp. 405-421.

31. This would be a welcome option, as Orthodox and Protestants object to the absence of synodality among Catholics.

32. St Catherine of Siena may have brought the Pope back to Rome, but that didn't reform the papacy, and we got the Reformation.

Part Four: Theological Forum

Pope Francis' Call for a New Economy

KLAUS DA SILVA RAUPP

The scenario in which the young Giovanni di Pietro Bernardone lived in the small town of the beautiful region of Umbria, in Italy, whom the world later knew as Francis of Assisi, was not exactly the current one, since he did not live in a time of predominance of the Capitalist economic mode of production. However, there was already a breakdown of the feudal system, with a newborn bourgeoisie and the consequent transition to Capitalism. The movie "Francesco", directed by Italian filmmaker Liliana Cavani, describes very well the poverty and human/social degradation that plagued Assisi and the region at the end of the 12th century.

It is in this scenario that the young son of the rich merchant, courted in various ways in his privileges, and at the same time disturbed by the war and its horrors, listened to the words that converted his life and those of so many people after him (the famous moment he had in front of the painted Byzantine crucifix in the small church of San Damian): "Go, Francis, and rebuild my church, which, as you see, falls into ruins" (see Thomas of Celano 13; 2C 10, in the Franciscan Sources). A conversion that made him walk on the direction of perfect joy, having "Poverty Lady" as his companion, and opening his existence to a relational and ethical way that, as known, ultimately translated into an effective canticle to God and all the creatures.

In 2013, coming from the "end of the world", Cardinal Jorge Mario Bergoglio, Jesuit, Archbishop of Buenos Aires, and heir to the Latin American tradition of Argentine "flavour" (the theology of the people or culture), assumed the Chair of Peter as Bishop of Rome and Pope of the

Catholic Church. After a brief conversation with Brazilian Cardinal Claudio Hummes ("don't forget the poor"), which followed the final moments of the conclave, and about to present himself to Rome and the world at the balcony in front of the people in St. Peter's Square, Bergoglio decided to call himself Francis. He said that he intended to walk with the people, and asked them to pray for his bishop before granting the *urbi et orbi* apostolic blessing. In the same year, in the Apostolic Exhortation after the Synod for the Evangelization, he made it very clear in the second chapter of this document (which can be said as a program of his pontificate): this economy kills, and needs to be denied. The Pope stated: "we must say no to an economy of exclusion and social inequality" (*Evangelii gaudium,* n. 53).

Pope Francis has then dedicated special attention to the peripheries of the world and of existence, in a context of poverty and human social degradation that, already in the 21st century, still plague us, and on an increasing scale. Francis started to dialogue intensively with the popular movements, highlighting the need for a new economy and, as João Pedro Stédile emphasized, "a process of articulation in a world level that can lead, more than to outline unitary programs, to develop actions and mobilizations that, at the international level, really face the problems caused by Capitalism". An economy that guarantees universal access to land, housing, and work, and is not reduced to the logic of accumulation (which is inherent to the currently predominant economic mode of production). An economy based on the principle of integral ecology, in the face of a single socio-environmental crisis, as stated in the Encyclical *Laudato Si'*. On this path, the Pope decided to summon the global youth to "establish a pact to change the current economy and assign a soul to the economy of tomorrow" at the common table in Assisi, that is, to "re-establish the economy"; a clear call for the Economy of Francesco.

In a very brief analysis of conjuncture, and also of this call, it seems urgent that some minimal consensus be planted around objective reality (what we perceive as a ruined economy), and the meaning of the words (what we understand about Pope Francis' call to the youth around the world). With regard to the perception of reality (and with honesty in relation to what is real – Jon Sobrino), it is worth highlighting the value of tools such as the world-system analysis, in its understanding of both the global and the local perspectives, and of the so-called long term. And, with these tools in hand, the following is also urgent: to realize that, despite the redundancy, Capitalism is an economic mode of production characterized by laws immanent to the regime of Capital (which, among many others, contemplates hidden realities such as surplus value), and not to free market itself; to make clear that, in Capitalism, class struggle is a given, and not a preaching of those who oppose it, and that accumulation / centralization / concentration of capital are immanent trends, as said; plus, to affirm that Capitalism, in its current stage (neoliberal and financial), is incompatible with liberal democracy itself (something that had already been anticipated by Karl Polanyi in the 1940s), and is currently leading us to the end of the age of humanism (as recently suggested by Achilles Mbembe). Therefore, a new economy requires the overcoming of this model, which obviously involves sociological, political, cultural, technological, and other aspects to be considered globally, as well as local actions based on a territorial organization of social actors.

With regard to understanding the call made by Pope Francis, it is worth mentioning that his message recovers the impulse of Vatican Council II to "return to the sources", which refers, among others: to the historical-critical understanding of the Scriptures (which are abundant in the narratives in favour of a liberating reading of the conditions of oppression – see the experience of Moses and the exodus, the announcement and denunciation of the prophets, the mission of Jesus according to Luke, the way of life of the first Christian communities, etc.); to an understanding of the Church's social teaching, and also of its practice, as central to her own creed (the Catechism itself states that a theory that makes profit the exclusive rule and the ultimate end of economic activity is morally unacceptable, and that the Church rejects, in the practice of capitalism, individualism and the absolute primacy of the market law on human labour – paragraphs 2424 and 2425); in this sense, to the understanding that the common good, the universal destination of goods (and the consequent preferential option for the poor), etc. are guiding principles of Catholic thinking and acting, but, of course, not restricted to the Catholic world, as per the Pope's call for the meeting in Assisi and the process that it originated.

In his Letter to the "Economy of Francesco" event, Francis wrote that he wanted to meet with the young people "to promote together, through a common pact, a process of global change that sees in communion of intentions not only how many have the gift of faith, but all men of good will, in addition to differences in creed and nationality, united by an ideal of fraternity attentive above all to the poor and the excluded". The Pope wants the young people to play a leading role, therefore, and invited them to "[assume] an individual and collective commitment to cultivate together the sign of a new humanism that corresponds to man's expectations and God's plan". In other words, just as the crucified Christ "spoke" to Francis of Assisi, Francis of Rome speaks to the young people all over the world: "Go, young people of Francis, and rebuild our economy, which, as you see, falls into ruins!".

In the face of the current pandemic, the event was rescheduled and initially took place in an online format in November 19-21, 2020, but is still meant to happen in Assisi around the same time in 2021. In addition to participating in some conferences on central themes, the young people have been invited to meet in twelve thematic villages in order to contribute to the task of thinking about the new economy, and thus answer the Pope's call. They are: Agriculture and justice; Business and peace; Business in transition; CO^2 of inequalities; Economy and Women; Energy and poverty; Finance and humanity; Life and Lifestyle; Management and gift; Policies & Happiness; Profit and Vocation; and Work and care. However, more important than the event itself is the process that has already been started since the original call (and reinforced by himself in the message to participants in the virtual meeting), which has even given rise to many articulations that seek the construction of concrete paths on the direction pointed out by Francis. [1]

Note

1. The text of this article corresponds to the author's contribution to the inaugural article of the weekly column "Towards the Economy of Francesco" published by the IHU portal, which is an initiative of Unisinos, the biggest Jesuit University in Brazil.

Contributors

CELIA ROJAS CHÁVEZ – Good Shepherd sister. She began her Church journey in Chiapas in July 1987 and has lived her service among the Maya Tseltal and Tsotsil peoples for 27 years.

Email: celia2117@hotmail.com

DR JULIA KNOP is professor of dogmatic theology at the University of Erfurt.

Address: Katholisch-Theologische Fakultät der Universität Erfurt, Lehrstuhl für Dogmatik, Nordhäuser Str. 63 - Villa Martin, 99089 Erfurt Germany
Email: julia.knop@uni-erfurt.de

DR. MARTIN KIRSCHNER is Professor of Theology in Transformation Processes of the Present at the Eichstätt-Ingolstadt Catholic University and directs its Religion, Church, Changing Society centre.

Address: Katholische Universität Eichstätt-Ingolstadt, Theologische Fakultät, Pater-Philip-Jeningen-Platz 6, D-85072 Eichstätt, Germany
Email: kirschner@ku.de

DR KOCHURANI ABRAHAM is an Indian feminist theologian, who is committed to addressing justice concerns through the academia and in grassroots engagements. She was the National Convener of ICWM and is at present the Vice President of the Indian Theological Association (ITA).

Address: Kochurani Abraham, 9A Veegaland Kings Town, Thripunithura P.O, Kochi, Kerala-682 301, India
Email: kochuabraham@gmail.com

AGENOR BRIGHENTI Doctor of Theological and Religious Science, The Catholic University of Louvain: Research Professor at the PUC, Curitiba and visiting professor of the Instituto Teológico-Pastoral of the Latin American Episcopal Council, Bogotá; Member of the Theological Reflection Team at CELAM. Former expert advisor for CELAM at the Santo Domingo Conference of the National Conference of Brazilian Bishops, both in Aparecida and at the Amazon Synod.

Email: agenor.brighenti@pucpr.br

BARBARA E. REID OP holds a Ph.D. in Biblical Studies from The Catholic University of America in Washington, D.C. She is Carroll Stuhlmueller, CP Distinguished Professor of New Testament Studies and President of Catholic Theological Union. She is General Editor of *Wisdom Commentary* series, written by feminist biblical scholars and published by Liturgical Press.

Address: Catholic Theological Union, 5401 S. Cornell Ave., Chicago, IL 60615, USA

Email: breid@ctu.edu

STAN CHU ILO is a Research Professor of World Christianity and African studies at the Center for World Catholicism and Intercultural Theology, DePaul University, Chicago; principal convener of the Pan-African Catholic Congress on Theology, Society and Pastoral Life; honorary Professor at Durham University, England. Recently published: *Church and Development in Africa (2014); A Poor and Merciful Church (2018); Wealth, Health, and Hope in African Christian Religion;* (2019), and *Someone Beautiful to God: Finding the light of Faith in a Wounded World* (2020), co-editor of *Faith in Action in Africa.*

Address: 3020 North 76th Court, Elmwood Park, IL, 60707, USA

Email: stanchuilo@yahoo.com

ALPHONSE BORRAS is a priest of the diocese of Liège (Belgium), and professeur emeritus of canon law at the Catholic University of Louvain. Among other things he has taught at the Brussels Institut d'Études théologiques and the Institut catholique de Paris. A specialist in penal canon law, he has also published in other areas of canon law, as well as in ecclesiology and the theology of ministry. He is currently working on *Libérer l'appel à la prêtrise*, to be published shortly by éditions Médiaspaul (Paris-Montréal).

Address: Rue de l'évêché, 25,B–4000 Liège, Belgium
Email: alphonse.borras@uclouvain

GILLES ROUTHIER is professor at Laval University, Quebec, where he holds the Monseigneur de Laval Chair and teaches ecclesiology and practical theology. His thesis on synodality in the local Church was completed at the Institut catholique de Paris in 1991.

Address: Faculté de théologie et de sciences religieuses, Pavillon Félix-Antoine-Savard, bureau 730, Université Laval, Québec, CANADA G1V 0A6
Email: gilles.Routhier@ftsr.ulaval.ca

RICHARD R. GAILLARDETZ is the Joseph Professor of Catholic Systematic Theology at Boston College. He is the editor of *The Cambridge Companion to Vatican II* (New York: Cambridge University Press, 2020).

Address: Richard R. Gaillardetz, 116 Furbush Rd. West Roxbury, MA, USA
Email: gaillard@bc.edu

CARLOS SCHICKENDANTZ has a doctorate in theology from the Eberhard-Karls-Universität Tübingen, Germany. He is a professor and researcher at the Centro Teológico Manuel Larraín, Universidad Alberto Hurtado, Santiago, Chile.

A list of his publications can be found at https://uahurtado.academia.edu/CarlosSchickendantz .

Address: Profesor Carlos Schickendantz, Universidad Alberto Hurtado, Alameda 1869, Santiago, Chile
Email: carlosschickendantz@gmail.com

HERVÉ LEGRAND OP (born in France in 1935) studied in the faculties of Le Saulchoir, Walberberg/Bonn, at the Angelicum University in Rome and in Strasbourg and Athens. He is an honorary professor of the Institut Catholique de Paris, has been an expert of the Conference of European

Bishops Conferences and in particular a member of the commission for dialogue between the Catholic Church and the World Lutheran Federation. His publications deal essentially with the Church, ministries and ecumenism.

Address: 20, rue des Tanneries, F-75013 Paris, France
Email: hervelegrandop@yahoo.fr

KLAUS DA SILVA RAUPP is a PhD Candidate in Theology and Education at Boston College (USA). His main research now is about the curriculum of Catholic Religious Education with focus on economic justice (and its intersections with Catholic Social Teaching, Liberation Theology, Social Reconstructionism, Critical Pedagogy, etc.). He is also an Attorney-at-Law in Brazil since 1998, holds a Master's degree in Systematic Theology from the Pontifical Catholic University of Rio Grande do Sul (Brazil), and has been teaching in the theological field since 2007. Currently, he is directly contributing to the process of the event "The Economy of Francesco", and is involved in pastoral work in the Archdiocese of Boston (USA).

Address: 2403 Main Campus Dr, Lexington, MA 02421 USA
Email: raupp@bc.edu

CONCILIUM

International Journal of Theology

PUBLISHERS

SCM Press (London, UK)
Matthias-Grünewald Verlag (Ostfildern, Germany)
Editrice Queriniana (Brescia, Italy)
Editorial Verbo Divino (Estella, Spain)
EditoraVozes (Petropolis, Brazil)

Concilium Secretariat:

Couvent de l'Annonciation
222 rue du Faubourg Saint-Honoré
75008 – Paris (France)
secretariat.concilium@gmail.com

Managing Editor: Gianluca Montaldi FN

https://concilium-vatican2.org

Concilium Subscription Information

July **2021/3:** *Incarnation*

October **2021/4:** *Amazons/Congo*

December **2021/5:** *End of Life*

February **2022/1:** *Theology in Asia*

April **2022/2:** *Covid-19*

New subscribers: to receive the next five issues of Concilium please copy this form, complete it in block capitals and send it with your payment to the address below. Alternatively subscribe online at www.conciliumjournal.co.uk

Please enter my annual subscription for Concilium starting with issue 2021/3.

Individuals
____ £52 UK
____ £75 overseas and (Euro €92, US $110)

Institutions
____ £75 UK
____ £95 overseas and (Euro €120, US $145)

Postage included – airmail for overseas subscribers

Payment Details:
Payment can be made by cheque or credit card.
a. I enclose a cheque for £/$/€ _____ Payable to Hymns Ancient and Modern Ltd
b. To pay by Visa/Mastercard please contact us on +44(0)1603 785911 or go to www.conciliumjournal.co.uk

Contact Details:
Name ....
Address ....
....
Telephone .... E-mail ....

Send your order to *Concilium*, **Hymns Ancient and Modern Ltd**
13a Hellesdon Park Road, Norwich NR6 5DR, UK
E-mail: concilium@hymnsam.co.uk
or order online at www.conciliumjournal.co.uk

Customer service information
All orders must be prepaid. Your subscription will begin with the next issue of Concilium. If you have any queries or require Information about other payment methods, please contact our Customer Services department.

www.ingramcontent.com/pod-product-compliance
Ingram Content Group UK Ltd.
Pitfield, Milton Keynes, MK11 3LW, UK
UKHW041645190726
13854UKWH00006B/2701

9 780334 031581